Name _____

The Alphabet

____ a line to connect the dots. Follow the letters of the alphabet.

Start here.

Name _____

Under-Cover Work

Color the pictures. Then cut them out and glue onto Ira's sleeping bag in ABC order.

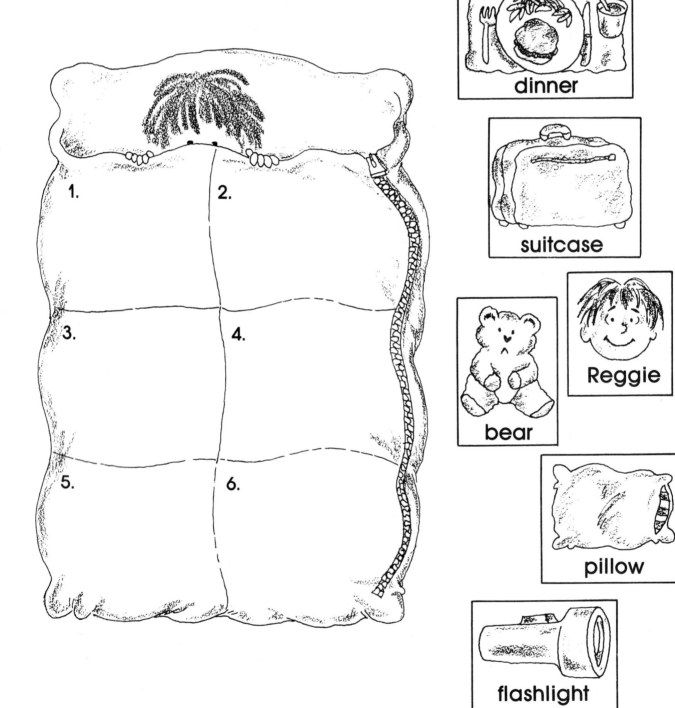

Name _____

The Quail Trail

Read the words. Cut and paste them on the quails in alphabetical order.

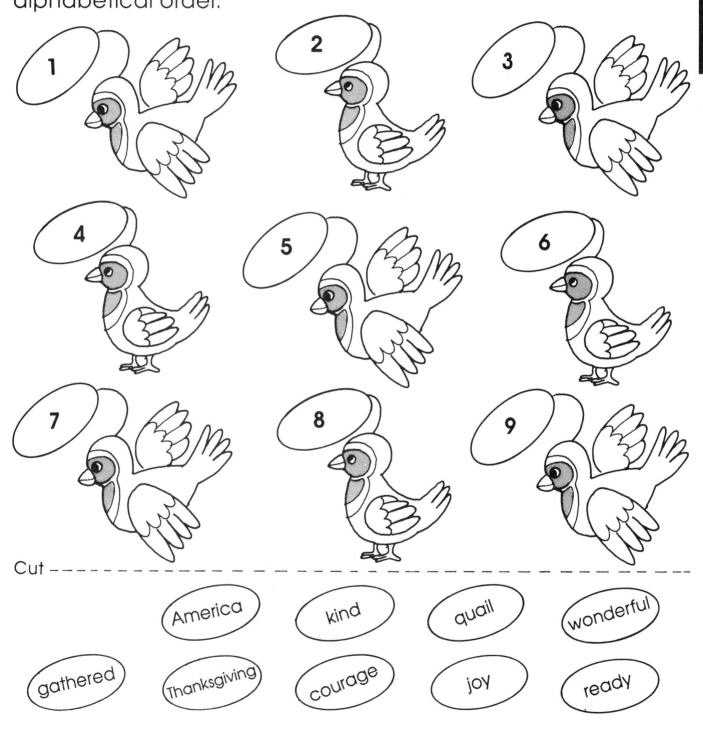

Cut -

America   kind   quail   wonderful

gathered   Thanksgiving   courage   joy   ready

Name _____

Squeeze a Summer Sipper

Read the words on the juicer. Write them in alphabetical order.

Word Bank

school	apples	leaves
working	playing	blossoms
town	clothes	mowing

1. _____

2. _____

3. _____

4. _____

5. _____

6. _____

7. _____

8. _____

9. _____

Name _____

Morris Learns the Alphabet

To help Morris find his way to the candy store write the words from the Word Bank in ABC order.

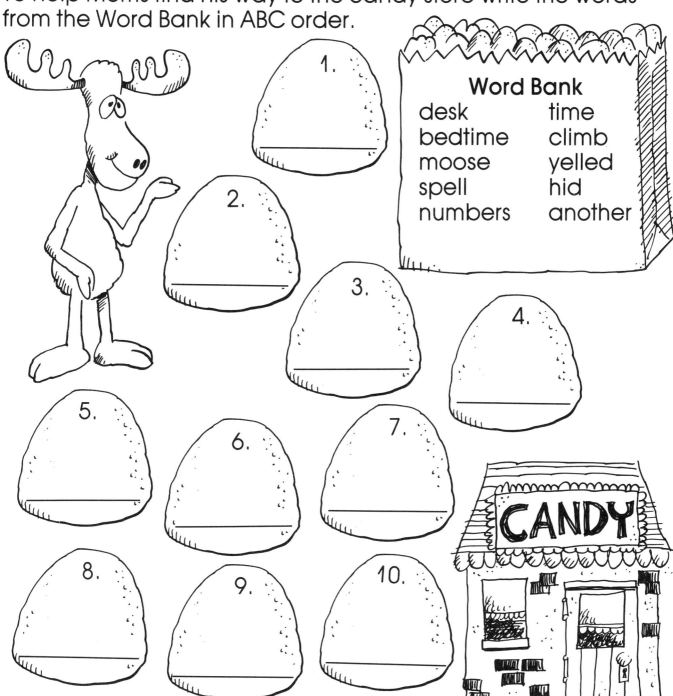

Word Bank

desk	time
bedtime	climb
moose	yelled
spell	hid
numbers	another

1.
2.
3.
4.
5.
6.
7.
8.
9.
10.

Candy Store

Name _____

Ghosts and Spaceships

Write the words in ABC order on the correct picture.

Color space word boxes red and blue.
Color Halloween word boxes orange and black.

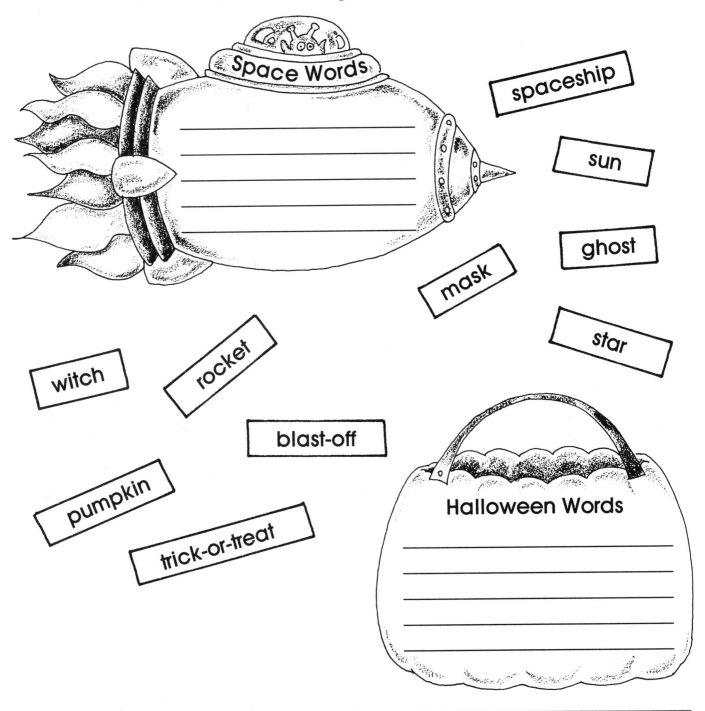

Name _____

Alpha-bear-tical Antics

Follow the directions to answer the riddle below. In each paw, print the letter that comes...

1. Between H and J

6. Before S

2. After G

7. After K

3. Before N

8. Before B

4. After A

9. Between D and F

5. Between S and U

Now answer the riddle by writing the letter from each paw print in the space above the same number.

Riddle

What famous lady bear was the first to fly across the Atlantic Ocean?

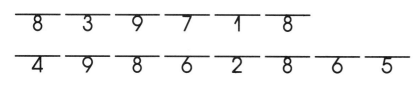

—— —— —— —— —— ——
 8   3   9   7   1   8

—— —— —— —— —— —— —— ——
 4   9   8   6   2   8   6   5

Name _____

Letter Lift

Cut out the letter squares. Paste each square on the correct balloon.

| o | s | m | a | q | h | d | o | r | j | x | p |
| f | g | t | i | l | b | e | n | v | u | c | k |

Name _____

"Feast" Your Eyes on This!

Look at the picture. Find and circle the letters that are hidden in the picture that spell **Happy Thanksgiving**. Color the picture.

LANGUAGE ARTS

Name _____

Sea Search

Help the boat sail to the island! Color the fish:

capital letters—orange **lower-case letters**—blue

Take One or Two

Name _____

Look at each picture on the cookies and read the word below it. Cut and paste each cookie on the correct jar to show how many syllables are in the word.

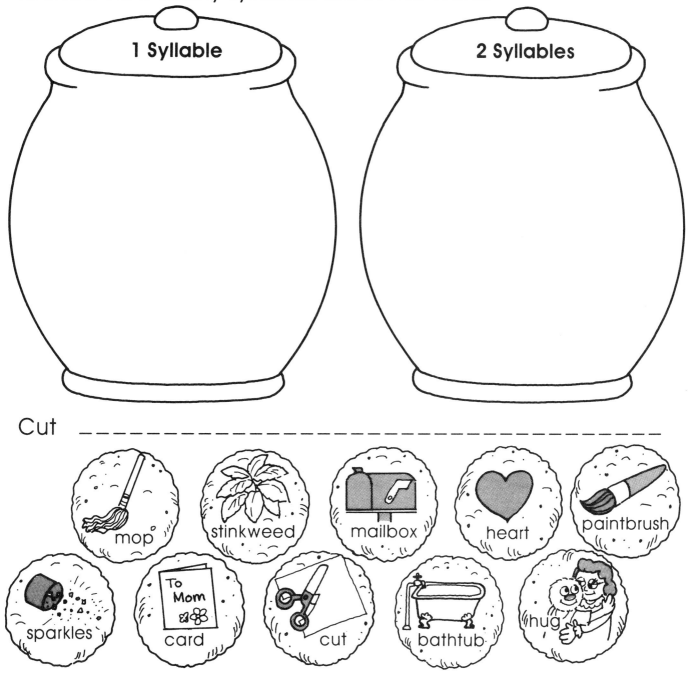

1 Syllable

2 Syllables

Cut _____

mop stinkweed mailbox heart paintbrush

sparkles card cut bathtub hug

11 IF8693 Super Book for Grade 1

Name _____

Two for the Dragon

Cut out the muffins. Glue the six muffins with two-syllable words on the dragon's tummy. Glue the rest in the center of another sheet of drawing paper. Then create and color your own dragon around these muffins.

king

poor

drawbridge

dragon

firewood

muncher

flour

bake

kingdom

villagers

bowl

muffin

Bonus

Fill these muffins with your own two-syllable words.

     IF8693 Super Book for Grades 1

Name _____

Half a Zoo

McGrew needs your help to capture the other half of these new zoo animals. Draw a matching half for each picture on this page. Color.

Elephant-Cat

Obsk

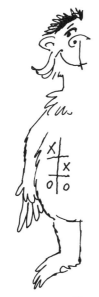

Tick-Tack-Toe

Iota

Name _____

Warm and Cozy

Look at the picture very carefully. All of the animals are snuggled in different places. Circle the eight animals hidden in the picture. Then color the picture.

rabbit   badger   duck   mouse

mole   hedgehog   fox   squirrel

Name _____

Hidden Pebble Search

Sylvester hid 20 magic pebbles in this picture. Find the pebbles. Color them red and circle them with black. Then color the rest of the picture.

Name _____

Snowy Day

Circle the mistakes in this crazy, snowy-day picture. Then color all parts of the picture.

Name _____

Select a Synonym

Read the words. ✎ the word that means almost the same as the first word.

1. big	cold	loud	large
2. yell	shout	eat	jump
3. small	good	thin	little
4. smile	tall	grin	soft
5. boat	talk	ship	hop
6. look	see	fall	laugh

Name _____

Similar Meanings

Read the words in the word box.  two words under each picture.

rock	start	road	begin	street	stone
shut	sad	talk	unhappy	speak	closed

_____

Name _____

A Change in the Weather

Change Alexander's cloudy day into a sunny day! Cut and paste an opposite in the ☀ for each ☁ word.

  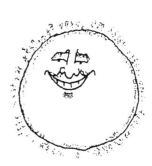

   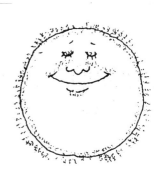

Word Bank

happy   play   night   cold   outside

       IF8693 Super Book for Grade 1

Name _____

Attach an Antonym

Read the word on each person. Find the word above the hair that means the opposite and paste it on that head.

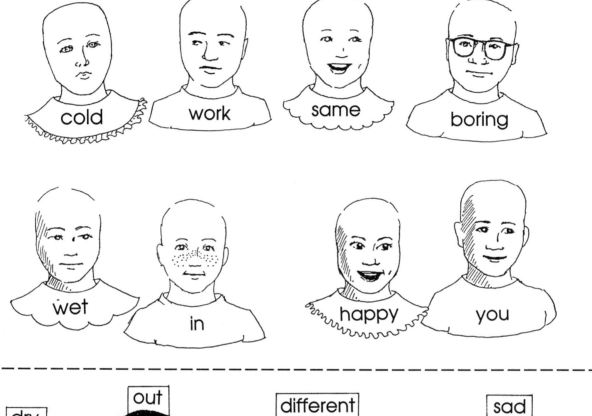

cold   work   same   boring

wet   in   happy   you

Cut --

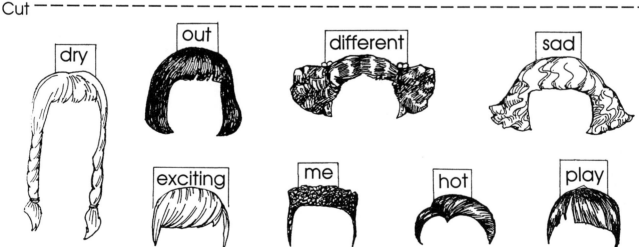

dry   out   different   sad

exciting   me   hot   play

Name _____

In or Out?

Read the words. Find a word in the Word Bank that means the opposite of each word given. Then write it on the line.

1. up _____
2. in _____
3. sad _____
4. stop _____
5. big _____
6. on _____
7. left _____
8. here _____
9. yes _____
10. mother _____

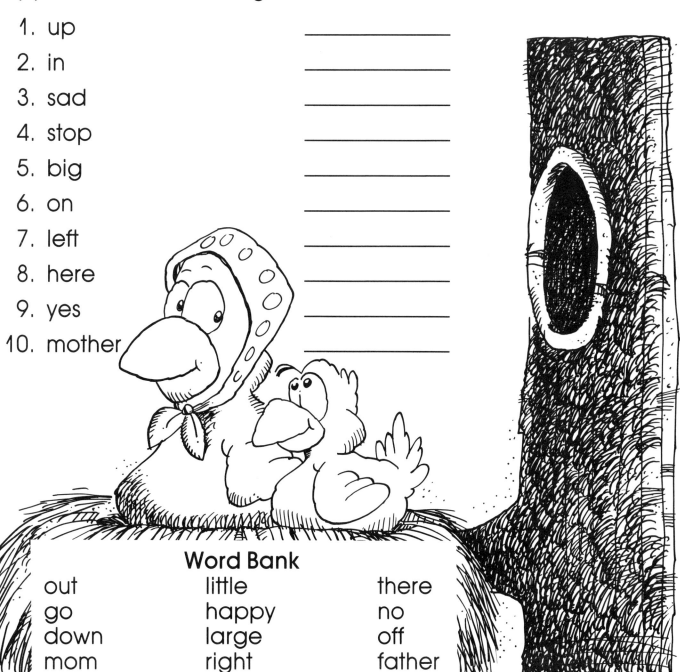

Word Bank

out	little	there
go	happy	no
down	large	off
mom	right	father

Name _____

Same or Opposite?

Color the spaces yellow that have word pairs with opposite meanings. Color the spaces blue that have word pairs with the same meanings.

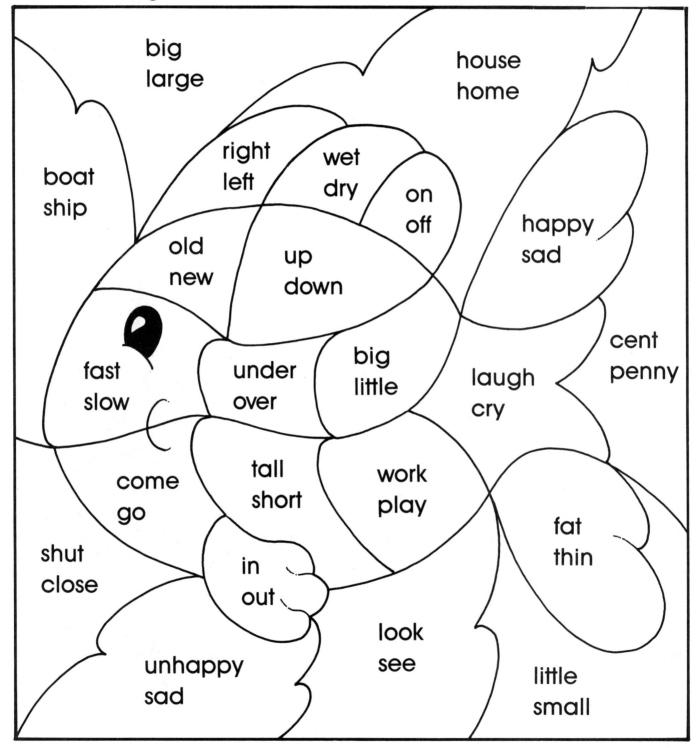

big
large

house
home

boat
ship

right
left

wet
dry

on
off

happy
sad

old
new

up
down

cent
penny

fast
slow

under
over

big
little

laugh
cry

come
go

tall
short

work
play

fat
thin

shut
close

in
out

look
see

unhappy
sad

little
small

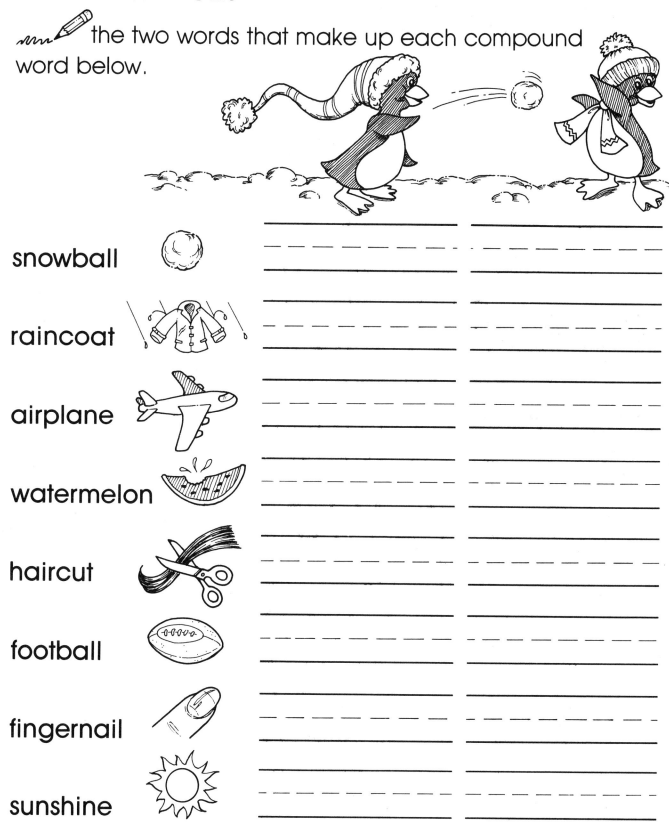

Name _____

Two Words in One

the two words that make up each compound word below.

snowball

raincoat

airplane

watermelon

haircut

football

fingernail

sunshine

Name _____

It's Raining Meatballs!

Draw a line from each word in List A to a word in List B to make a compound word. On another piece of paper, write the compound words and draw pictures of them.

List A

finger • pan • basket • dog • snow • rain • air • fish • flower

List B

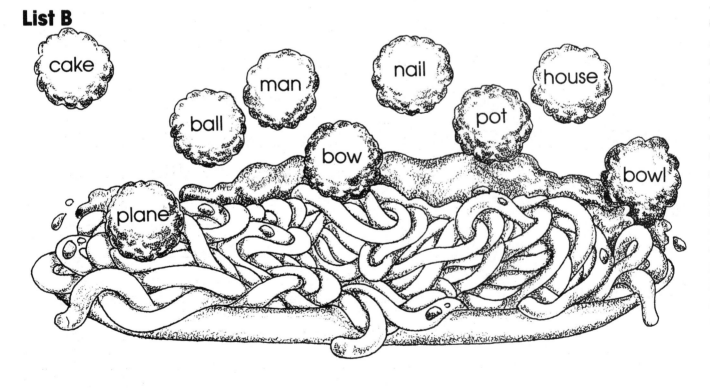

cake • man • nail • house • ball • pot • bow • bowl • plane

Name _____

"Compound"-ing the Cave's Echo

Read the words in the Word Bank. Find the two words that go together to make a compound word and write it on a bat.

bath	bed	bee
birth	by	comb
cow	day	every
fire	flies	for
got	grass	hide
hive	honey	lands
lights	near	
one	room	
spread	street	

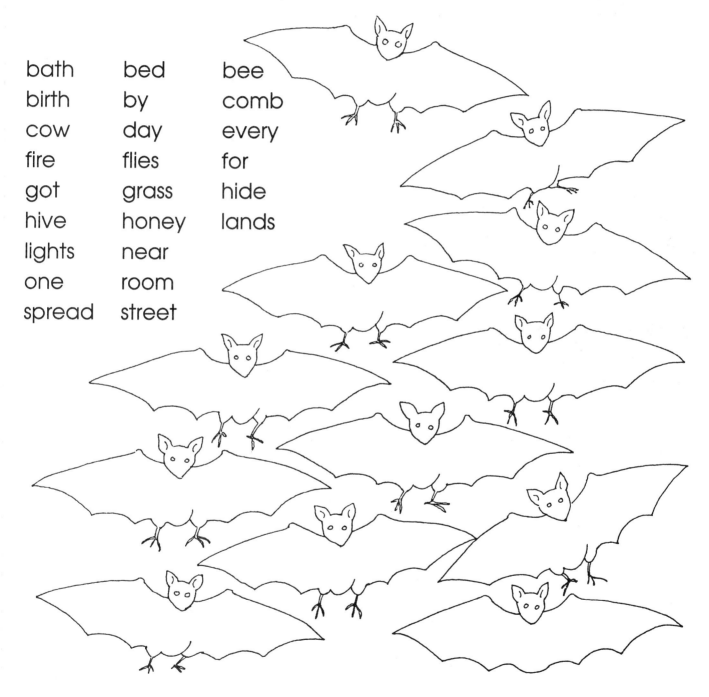

Name _____

Let's Make a Snowman

a line from each pair of words to the right contraction.

he is •   • it's

it is •   • she's

she is •   • he's

they are •   • you're

you are •   • they're

we are •   • I'm

I am •   • we're

Loppy Ears

Name _____

A contraction is a short way to write two words. Choose a contraction from the big carrot and print it on the lines.

1. Leo _____ get his ears to stand up tall.

2. _____ not fun to be teased by the others.

3. "_____ not normal," thought Leo.

4. Doing ear exercises _____ help Leo.

5. _____ go see the possum, he'll know what to do.

6. _____ my good friend.

7. The other bunnies _____ get their ears to flop down.

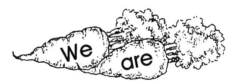

8. _____ all normal because we are loved.

I'm   We're   couldn't   can't   He's   didn't
I'll   It's

Name _____

"Crumb"-y Contractions

Read the two words on the bread crumbs. Find the contraction in the Word Bank and write it on the bird.

we   are

that   is

I   would

I   will

she   is

they   are

she   would

let   us

we   would

we'd   she's
let's   I'll
I'd   we're

they're
that's
she'd

Name _____

Barnyard Nouns

A noun is a naming word.
A noun names a person, place or thing.

Find **two** nouns in each sentence below.
 them.

1. The pig has a curly tail.	
2. The hen is sitting on her nest.	
3. A horse is in the barn.	
4. The goat has horns.	
5. The cow has a calf.	
6. The farmer is painting the fence.	

Name _____

Nouns on the Farm

Read the naming words below. ✏ the correct
naming word for each picture of a person, place
or thing.

barn	farmer	pig
boy	tree	horse
girl	ducks	sun

Name _____

Action Match

Find the action word in each sentence.  it.
 a line to match each sentence with the correct picture.

1. The dog barks.

2. The bird flies.

3. A fish swims.

4. One monkey swings.

5. A turtle crawls.

6. A boy talks.

Name _____

Circus Action

Find the verb in each sentence below and  it.

1. The bear climbs a ladder.

2. Two tiny dogs dance.

3. A boy eats cotton candy.

4. A woman swings on a trapeze.

5. The clown falls down.

6. A tiger jumps through a ring.

Name _____

Falling Verbs

only the leaves that have verbs.

read

rabbit

baby

hops

father

dig

fish

looked

truck

city

jumps

drank

walked

claps

Name _____

Am I a Noun or a Verb?

Color the spaces with **naming** words green. Color the spaces with **action** words pink.

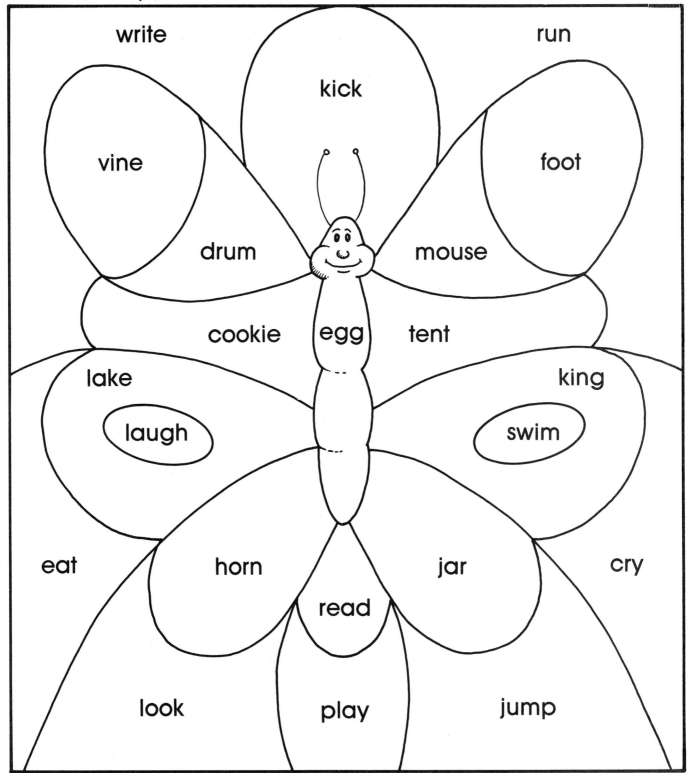

Name _____

Animal Adjectives

✏ a describing word in each sentence below.
Use the word bank to help you.

Word Bank

big
round

bushy
green

three
six

1. A has a _____ tail.

2. A has _____ legs.

3. The will become a _____ frog.

4. A has _____ teeth.

5. _____ hang by their tails.

6. An has _____ eyes.

Name _____

Fishing for Adjectives

 only the fish with describing words.

Name _____

Corn Crackles

Here are some describing words:

sour	furry	sweet	tasty	crisp
tall	crunchy	cloudy	sad	soft

Which four words do you think might best describe the cereal?  them on the lines on the cereal box.

Name _____

The Turtles Tell

> Some sentences tell something.
> Telling sentences begin with a capital letter.
> Telling sentences end with a period.

only the sentences that tell.

1. Two turtles sat on a log.

2. One turtle fell off.

3. Did you see him?

4. He swam away.

5. The water is cold.

6. Can you swim?

Name _____

All About Dinosaurs

✏️ the telling sentences below. Begin each sentence with a capital letter and end with a period.

1. dinosaurs lived long ago

_____

- -

_____

2. many were very big

_____

- -

_____

3. some dinosaurs ate plants

_____

- -

_____

4. all the dinosaurs died out

_____

- -

_____

5. no one is sure why

_____

- -

_____

Name _____

State It!

Some sentences tell something. They are called statements. A statement begins with a capital letter and ends with a period.

✏ these statements correctly.

1. jenny planted a seed

_____

2. she gave it water

_____

3. it sat in the sunshine

_____

4. the plant began to grow

_____

5. leaves grew large

_____

6. a flower opened

_____

Fishy Questions

Name _____

✏ the first word of each question below.
Remember to begin with a capital letter. End each
question with a question mark.

1. _____ that your boat__
   (is)

2. _____ you catch that fish__
   (did)

3. _____ much does it weigh__
   (how)

4. _____ you eat it__
   (will)

5. _____ you fish with worms__
   (did)

6. _____ the water cold__
   (is)

Name _____

Did You Ask Me Something?

Some sentences ask something. They are called questions. A question begins with a capital letter and ends with a question mark.

✏ only the questions.

1. Is that your house?

2. There are two pictures on the wall.

3. Where do you sleep?

4. Do you watch TV in that room?

5. Which coat is yours? _____

6. The kitten is asleep.

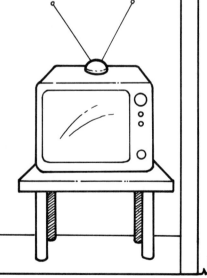

Name _____

Period or Question Mark?

Put a period or a question mark at the end of each sentence.

1. Can the fish jump out of the tank ☐

2. Two snakes are in that cage ☐

3. How much does that turtle cost ☐

4. Yes, I already have a dog ☐

5. His name is King ☐

6. Do you have a dog ☐

Name _____

What a Trick!

If the word names an animal, color the space **brown**.
If the word names something to eat, color the space **blue**.
If the word names something found in the sky, color the space **yellow**.
If the word names a piece of furniture, color the space **red**.
If the word names something you use in school, color the space **green**.

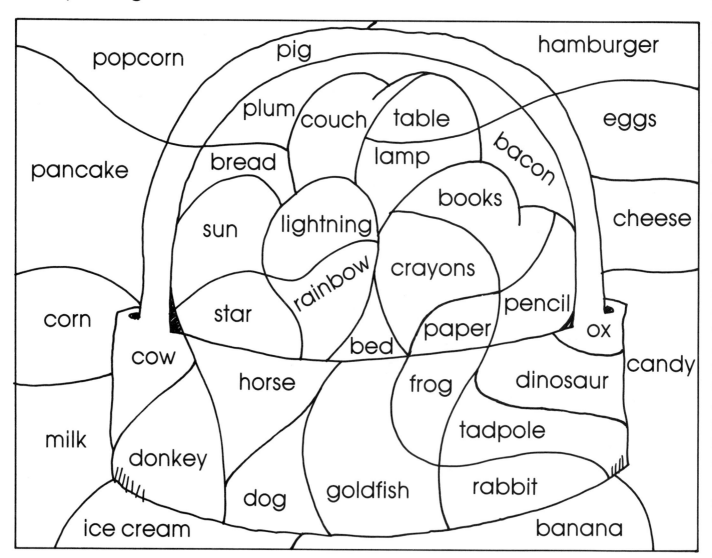

Name _____

Pick a Pouch

Cut and paste each word on the correct kangaroo pouch. Then color one kangaroo green and the other your favorite color.

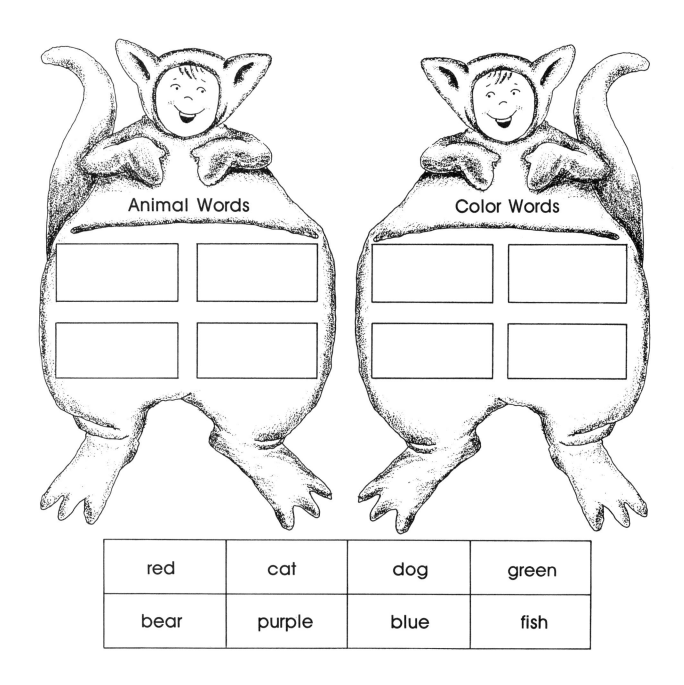

Animal Words

Color Words

red	cat	dog	green
bear	purple	blue	fish

"Cap" the Words

Name _____

Read the headings on the caps. Write the words from the Word Bank on the correct cap.

How Clothes Can Feel

_____
_____
_____
_____
_____

Words That Tell Where

_____
_____
_____
_____
_____

Which word is left over? _____

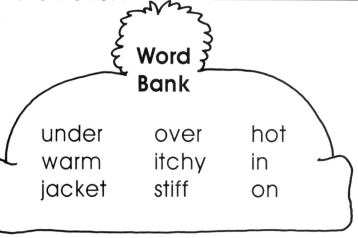

Word Bank

under	over	hot
warm	itchy	in
jacket	stiff	on

Name _____

Cake Faces

Cut and paste the words where they belong.

Names

Types of Costumes

Things That Are Fun

How Costumes Look

Cut ─

clown   Peter   party   Jenny   beautiful   monster

funny   games   princess   scary   playing   Billy

Name _____

Missing Pieces

Write the puzzle words on the correct lines. Color the pieces as shown.

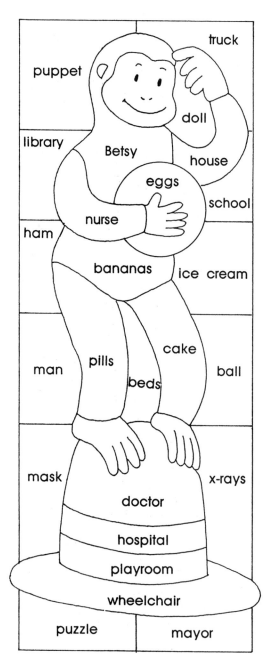

People purple

_____   _____

_____   _____

_____   _____

Things in a Hospital   red

_____   _____

_____   _____

Food   yellow

_____   _____

_____   _____

_____   _____

Places   green

_____   _____

_____   _____

Toys   blue

_____   _____

_____   _____

Name _____

Pumpkin Patch Pick

Read. Cut and paste each picture where it belongs.

The pumpkin is in the wagon.

The ladybug is on the sprout.

The butterfly is on the flower.

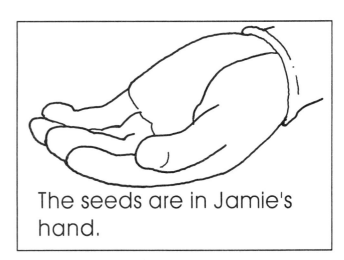

The seeds are in Jamie's hand.

Cut -

Name _____

Down on the Farm

A farm is a home for some animals. Horses, cows and pigs live on a farm. Sheep and chickens are farm animals, too. Many farm animals live in a big barn.

 Which animals live on a farm?

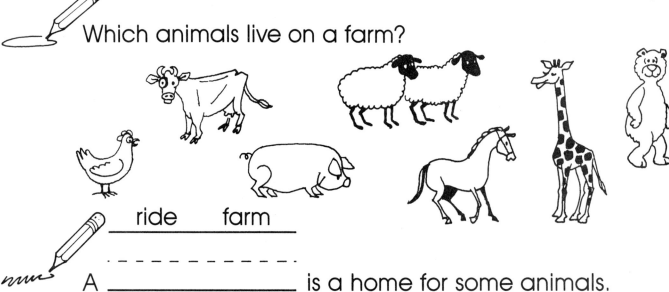

ride   farm

_____

- - - - - - - - - - -

A _____ is a home for some animals.

 Many farm animals live in a big

• Draw and color two farm animals.

barn.

Name _____

My Pet

It is fun to have a pet. Dogs and cats are good pets. Birds and rabbits can be pets, too. Pets are good friends. They need care and love every day.

friends   fast

_____

Pets are good _____ .

Pets need care and   long.
                              love.

| dog   rabbit   cat   bird |

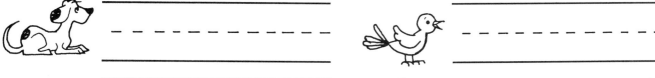

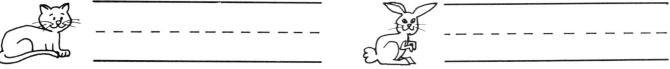

• Draw and color a picture of your pet.

Name _____

Mixed-up Colors

Did you know that all colors come from red, yellow or blue? They're the primary colors. Red and blue make purple. Blue and yellow make green. Yellow and red make orange. It is fun to mix paint to make new colors.

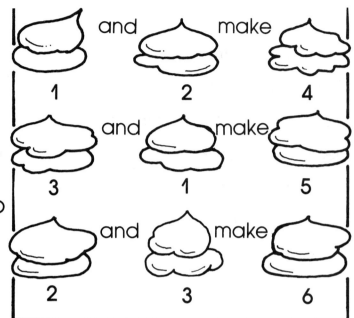

Circle.

Which three colors do you need to make all colors?

red   green   yellow   blue   pink

Write.

Red, yellow and blue are _____ colors.

orange   primary

Match.

Red and blue make   orange.

Blue and yellow make   purple.

Yellow and red make   green.

Color the picture: **1** - red   **2** - yellow   **3** - blue

                      4 - orange **5** - purple **6** - green

• Draw and color a picture using the **primary** colors.

Name _____

Scrambled Shoes

Minnie needs new shoes. She tries on several pairs and decides on one pair. Oops! While trying on all of the shoes, she has scattered them all over. Now she can't find the other shoe of the pair she wants.

Help Minnie find her shoe. Using a different color for each pair of shoes, color each pair exactly the same. Then draw a circle around Minnie's missing shoe.

Name _____

Barbecue Mishap

Meg and her family are barbecuing hamburgers. A gust of wind blows the flames toward a tree. Oh no! The tree is on fire! A fire truck races to the fire.

Trace the different ways the firefighters can get to Meg's house.

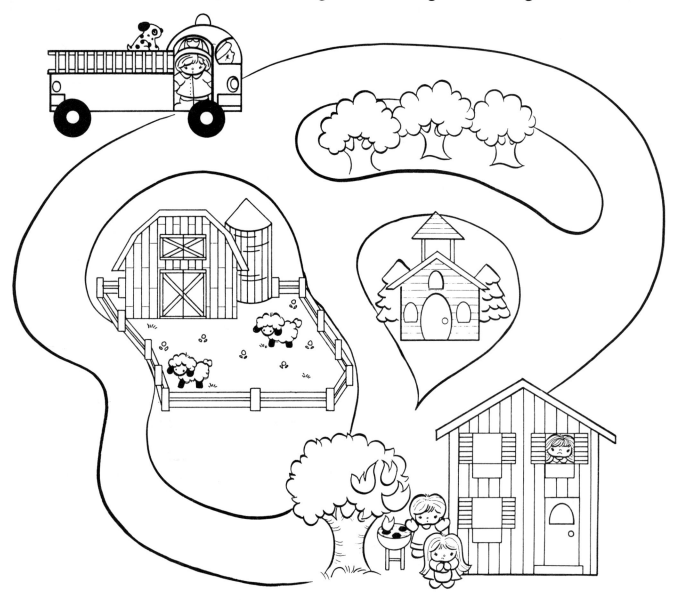

How many different ways did you find? _____

Use a red crayon to trace the quickest way to Meg's house.

Name _____

Musician's Choice

Many different instruments are used to make music. Irene knows how to play several musical instruments.

Irene knows how to play these instruments.

Irene does not know how to play these instruments.

Draw a circle around the instruments Irene probably also knows how to play.

Name _____

Family Portraits

Families may be big or small. No matter how many people are in a family, each person is important to the others.

Cut out the pictures at the bottom of the page. Read the clues. Paste the pictures of the members of this family in the frame where they belong.

- Grandfather is in the middle.
- The girl is on the right end.
- The boy is on the left end.
- Mother is between Grandmother and the boy.
- Father is beside the girl.
- The family dog is between Grandfather and Father.

Name _____

Where Is That Sheep?

Read. Cut and paste each sheep where it belongs. Color the pictures.

The sheep is on the table.	The sheep is under the loom.
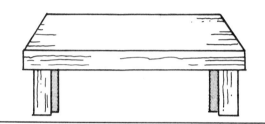	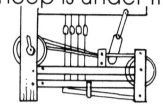
The sheep is in the pokeweed berry bush. 	The sheep is beside the cloth. 
The sheep is on Charlie's hat. 	The sheep is in between the pieces of Charlie's cloak. 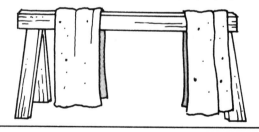

Cut —

IF8693 Super Book for Grade 1

Name _____

Umbrellas Up!

Look at the pictures. Circle the correct word and write it on the line.

Molly puts _____ the umbrella.

up   on   in

The tie is _____ the bed.

up   on   in

The cat is _____ the house.

up   on   in

The bird flies _____

up   on   in

He puts _____ mittens.

up   on   in

The dog is _____ the rain.

up   on   in

Name _____

Playing Parts

Look at each picture. Find the title of the story that Grace is acting out in the Word Bank. Write it under the correct picture.

_____

_____

_____

_____

_____

_____

Word Bank

The Case of the Missing Cat	Cowboy Jake & the Roundup
Space Adventures	The Lost Treasure Chest

Name _____

It's Time to . . .

✂ and 🖌 four sentences under the correct pictures.

Susie's alarm clock rings.

Susie picks up her books.

Susie is getting hungry.

Susie hears the school bell ring.

K k   R r

It's time to go home from school.   It's time to get up.

It's time to go to sleep.   It's time to go to school.

It's time to eat lunch.   It's time to paint the fence.

Name _____

What Will They Do?

Read each sentence and question. 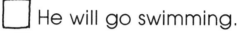 a ✓ in the box by the correct answer. a picture to answer the question.

Draw.

The boy is putting on his skates.

What will he do?

☐ He will go swimming.

☐ He will go skating.

Draw.

The girl fills her glass with milk.

What will she do?

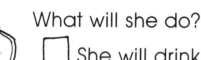

☐ She will drink the milk.

☐ She will drop the milk.

Draw.

The lady wrote a letter to her friend.

What will she do?

☐ She will throw the letter away.

☐ She will mail the letter.

Draw.

The kids gave Sally a birthday gift.

What will she do?

☐ She will open the gift.

☐ She will not open the gift.

LANGUAGE ARTS

Name _____

What Does That Mean?

Read. Color the picture that shows what each sentence **really** means.

We are just horsing around.

Pipe down, please.

The window flew open.

She had a puzzled look.

He is down in the dumps.

Save Six

Name _____

Color six animals.

Color six things that will grow.

Draw pictures of six of your favorite things on the back of this paper.

Name _____

Where's the Hair?

Draw different kinds of hair on each head. Color.

Suited for Winter

Name _____

Read and do.

1. Draw a hat on the snowman. Color the hat **purple** and **orange**.

2. Draw a snowsuit on the snowman. Color the snowsuit **blue.**

3. Draw boots on the snowman. Color the boots **yellow**.

4. Draw mittens on the snowman. Color the mittens **green**.

Name _____

Meet the Alien

1. Color the hands and arms yellow.
2. Print your name on the biggest ▭.
3. Draw a red ‿ on the face.
4. Put green dots on the ◠.
5. Color the purple.
6. Color all of the △'s orange.
7. Draw red and blue stripes on the legs ◯.
8. Color the □ blue.

Name _____

What's the Idea?

Read the sentence in each speech bubble. Underline the main idea.

My tummy hurts.

The mouse wants more to eat.
The mouse ate too much
cheese.

My hat is blowing away.

It is a very windy day.
He doesn't want a hat.

I am seven years old today.

The cake is very big.
Today is her birthday.

I can't find my home.

The cat is lost.
The cat has a new home.

May I have more ice cream?

She likes cake best.
She likes ice cream a lot.

Name _____

Yes or No?

Read each sentence. Circle **yes** if the sentence tells about the picture. Circle **no** if it does not.

yes   no

The running shoe is very old.

yes   no

The tree has lost its leaves.

yes   no

The soup smells good.

yes   no

Two butterflies sit on flowers.

yes   no

The dog eats a new bone.

yes   no

The boy sees the plane.

yes   no

The snake is lying on a rock.

yes   no

The spider is spinning its web.

Picture Pick

Name _____

Look at each picture. Read the sentences. the correct letter in each ○ to tell the main idea.

○ 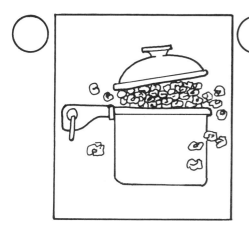   ○    ○

○    ○    ○

A- The eggs are ready to hatch.

B- It is a very windy day.

C- The old house is very spooky.

D- The popcorn popper is too full.

E- The girl thinks the music is too loud.

F- It is too warm for a snowman.

the pictures:
A — yellow
B — red
C — blue
D — green
E — orange
F — purple

IF8693 Super Book for Grade 1

Name _____

What About Bear?

Read each sentence. Circle **yes** if the sentence tells about the picture. Circle **no** if it does not.

yes   no

It is a very hot day.

yes   no

The hat is too small.

yes   no

The bear is afraid of the mouse.

yes   no

The bear washed three shirts.

yes   no

The circus is lots of fun.

yes   no

The bear has two mittens.

yes   no

The bear walks to school.

yes   no

The bear likes to cook.

        IF8693 Super Book for Grade 1

Name _____

What Did Morris Do Now?

Look at the pictures. Find the sentence in the Word Bank that matches each picture. Write it on the lines.

_____

_____

_____

_____

_____

_____

Word Bank

Morris hid his gumdrops.

Morris was too big for the desk.

Morris wanted to go home.

Morris was too little for the desk.

Morris pretended to be a closet.

71

Name _____

What a Life!

Read each sentence. If it tells something that could really happen, paste it under the real dog. If it tells something that is make-believe, paste it under the make-believe dog.

Cut -

A dog can fly a kite.	A dog can walk on a sidewalk.
A dog can sit beneath a tree.	A dog can be a lead singer.
A dog can splash in the water.	A dog puts jam on toast.
A dog can row a boat.	A dog likes to eat bones.

Name _____

My Friend the Bear

Read each sentence. If it tells something that could really happen, color the real bear. If it tells something that is make-believe, color the toy bear.

Real   **Make-Believe**

1. A bear can live in a forest.

2. A bear can search in a store for a lost button.

3. A girl can sew a button on a pair of overalls.

4. A bear can talk to a little girl.

5. A toy bear can ride up an escalator by himself.

6. A toy bear can sit on a toy department shelf.

7. A little girl can save money in a piggy bank.

8. A toy bear and a little girl can be friends.

9. A toy bear can yank a button off a mattress.

Go for the Snow

Read the word on each mitten. Find the word on a snowball that rhymes with it. Cut and paste the snowball on the correct mitten. Color the mittens.

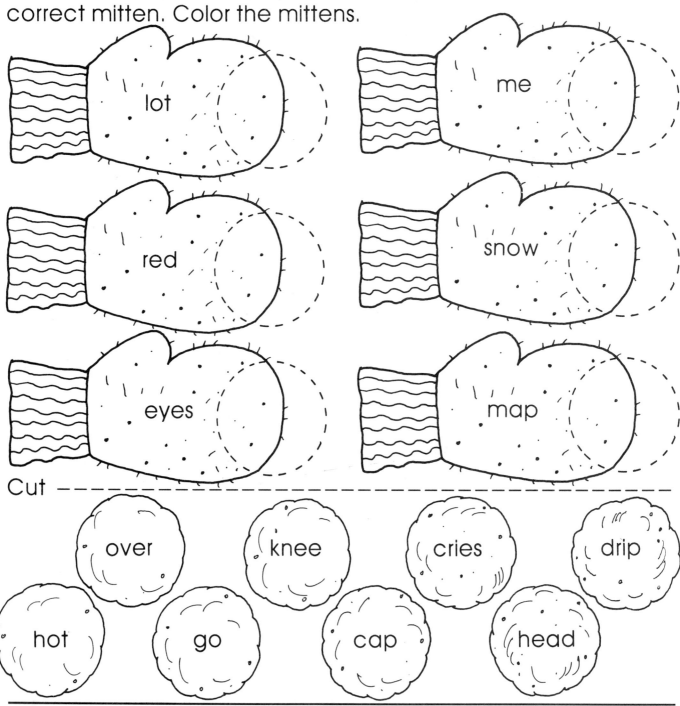

lot

me

red

snow

eyes

map

Cut -

over

knee

cries

drip

hot

go

cap

head

Name _____

Strawberry Patch Match

Read the word on each strawberry. Find the word in the
Word Bank that rhymes. Write it on the line.

sun _____

sky _____

bark _____

kite _____

flowers _____

Sam _____

day _____

goat _____

tea _____

cool _____

Word Bank

away	boat	high	fun
might	park	tree	jam
	showers		school

Name _____

A Space Case!

Read the word on each spaceship. Find the words in the Word Bank that rhyme and write them on the line.

two

small

most

rock

spotted

door

cat

me

funny

brown

Word Bank

fat	ghost	patch
tall	knock	clown
boo	three	dotted
step	four	bunny

Name _____

Carrot Crop

 the four pictures. ✂ and 🖌 the pictures in **1, 2, 3, 4** order.

Name _____

Fall Pick Up

Color the pictures. Cut and paste each picture in 1, 2, 3, 4 order.

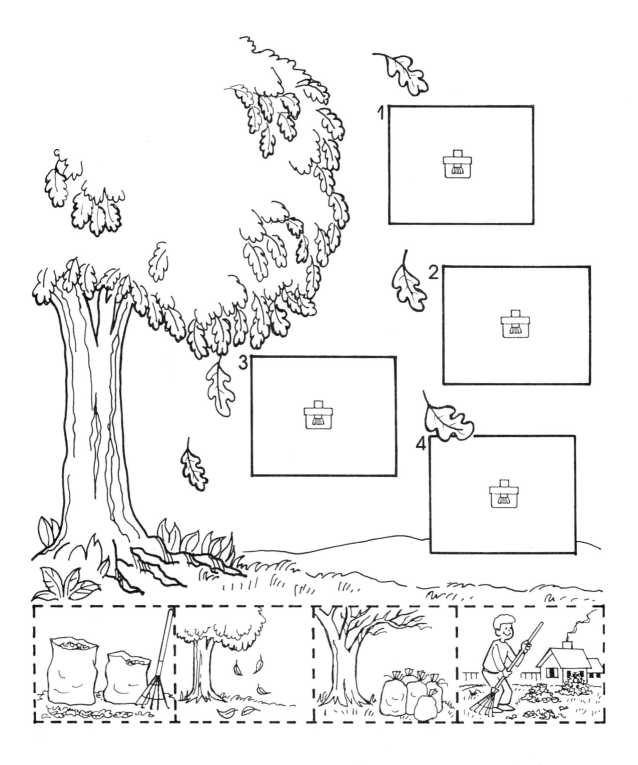

It's Hard to Wait!

Name _____

Write 1, 2, 3, or 4 in the boot next to the picture to show the order it happened in the story. Then draw a line from the boot to the sentence that tells about that picture.

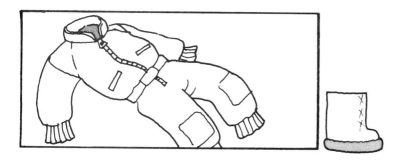

He has a new snowsuit.

He made a snowball.

He put on his new snowsuit, boots, hat and mittens.

He wished and wished for snow.

Name _____

How Many?

Read the words in the Word Bank. If the word means one, write it under Buster. If the word means more than one, write it under Sue Ellen.

one   more than one

1. _____ 1. _____

2. _____ 2. _____

3. _____ 3. _____

4. _____ 4. _____

5. _____ 5. _____

6. _____ 6. _____

Word Bank

teeth	child	class	people
straw	men	children	tooth
babies	person	recess	patients

LANGUAGE ARTS

Name _____

Animal Chatter

Unscramble the letters and  the name of each animal.
 the correct animal sound in each 🗨.

squeak   baa   gobble   moo   quack   meow   roar

o i l n _____

e m u o s _____

c d k u _____

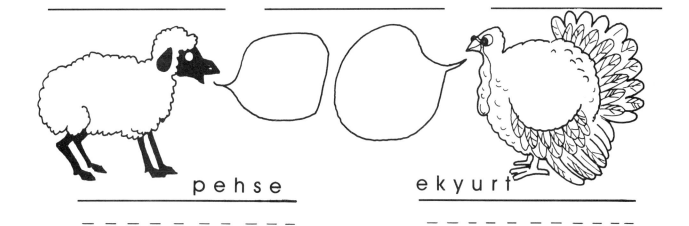

p e h s e _____

e k y u r t _____

w c o _____

t n i t k e _____

Size Search

Name _____

Circle each size word. Write the correct number by each picture. Color each picture the correct color.

1. a long, brown snake.

2. a little, red heart.

3. a tall, green tree.

4. a large, blue house.

5. a small, orange gift.

6. a short, yellow pencil.

7. a big, purple tent.

Name _____

Confection Perfection

Cut out the pictures of the candy at the bottom of the page. Paste the pictures to correctly continue the pattern in each row.

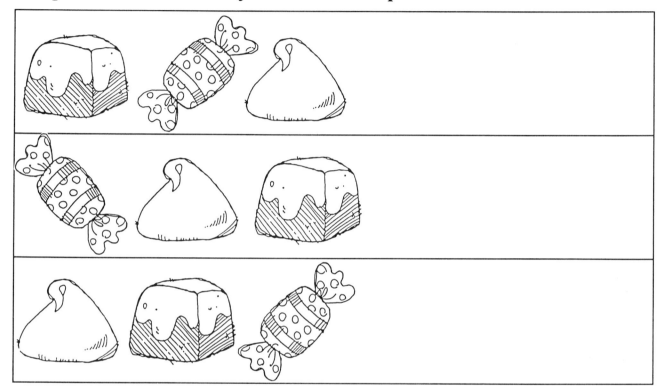

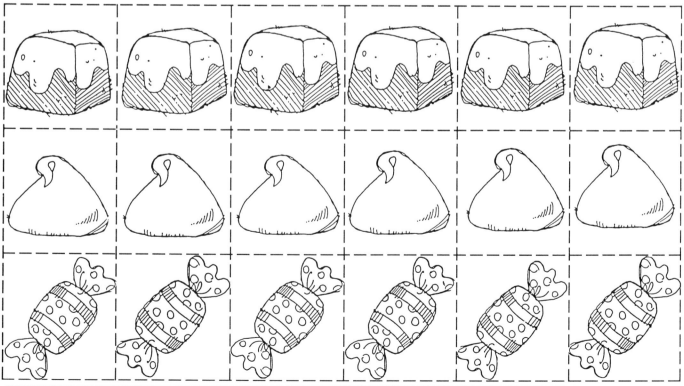

Name _____

Roaring Roller-Coaster Rides

Cut out the roller coaster cars at the bottom of the page. Paste them to correctly continue the pattern on each track.

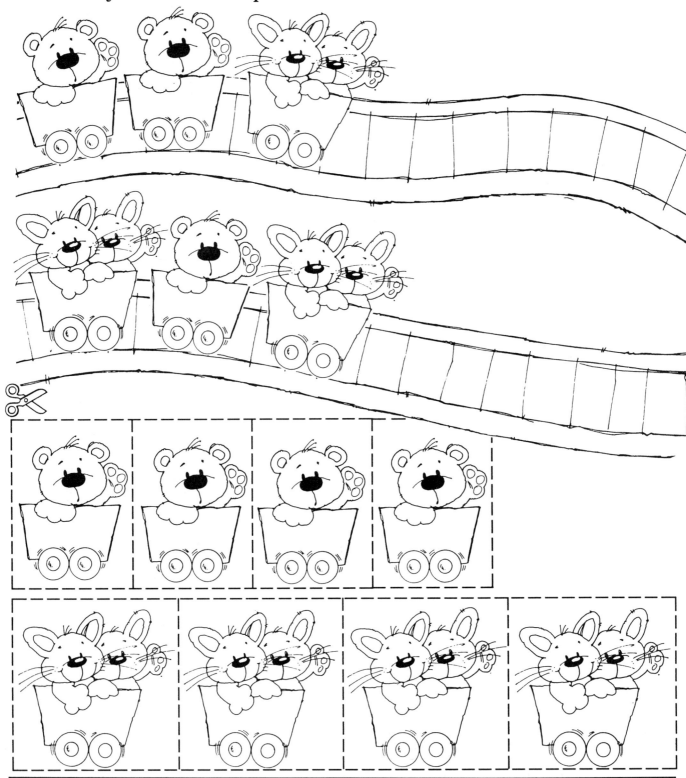

Name _____

Strawberry Stack-Up

Farmers grow ripe, red strawberries for everyone to eat. Before taking the strawberries to the stores, the farmers put them in small baskets.

Look at the pattern of the baskets in each row. Draw the correct number of strawberries in the baskets to continue each pattern.

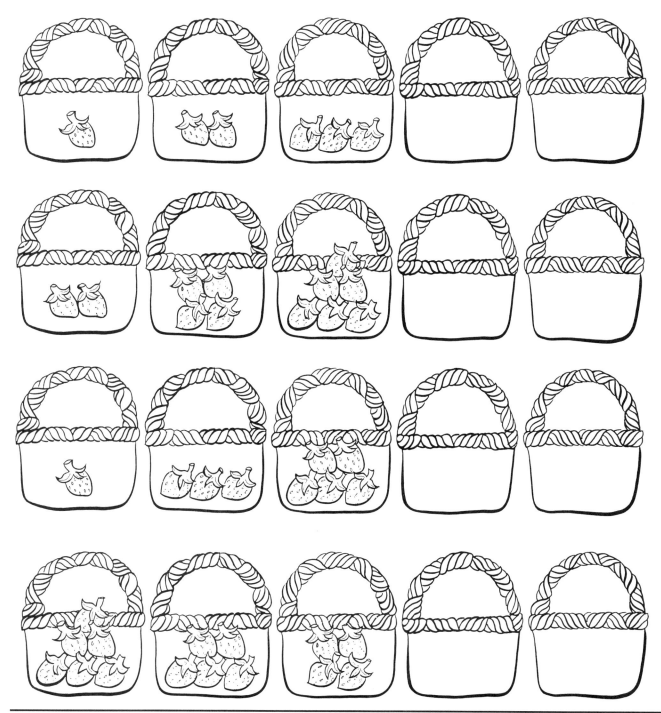

Stringing It Along

Name _____

Complete each pattern. Color the red and the pink.

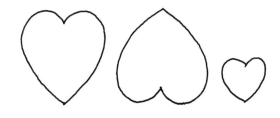

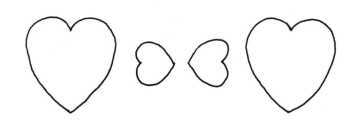

Name _____

Special Hearts for a Special Friend

Look at the picture carefully.

How many hearts were used to draw the cat? _____

Draw and color a picture of an animal using only heart shapes.

Name _____

Animal Action

Find the shapes and color the picture using the code.

⬤ red   ⬜ blue   ▭ yellow

△ green   ◇ orange   ⬭ black

Name _____

Cabin to Capitol

Abraham Lincoln was the 16th president of the United States. He was born in a log cabin. Many people lived in log cabins at that time.

Look at this picture of a log cabin. How many of each of the different shapes can you find in the picture?

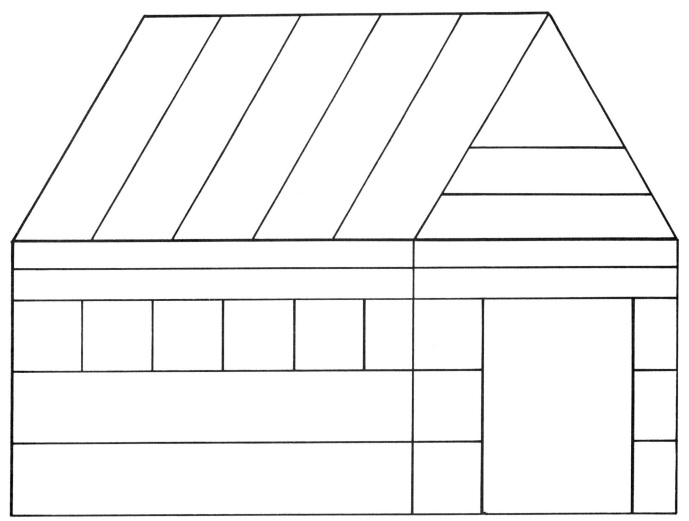

How many △ 's? _____

How many ▱ 's? _____

How many ☐ 's? _____

Draw and color a door.

Name _____

Mask Make-Up

Masks have been made by people for many years. In some countries, the actors in plays wear masks. Masks can be made from wood, metal, paper, cloth, or even foil. They can be painted with a design or a face. Color the mask by using the color code.

◯ **red**   ▢ **orange**   △ **yellow**   ▭ **blue**

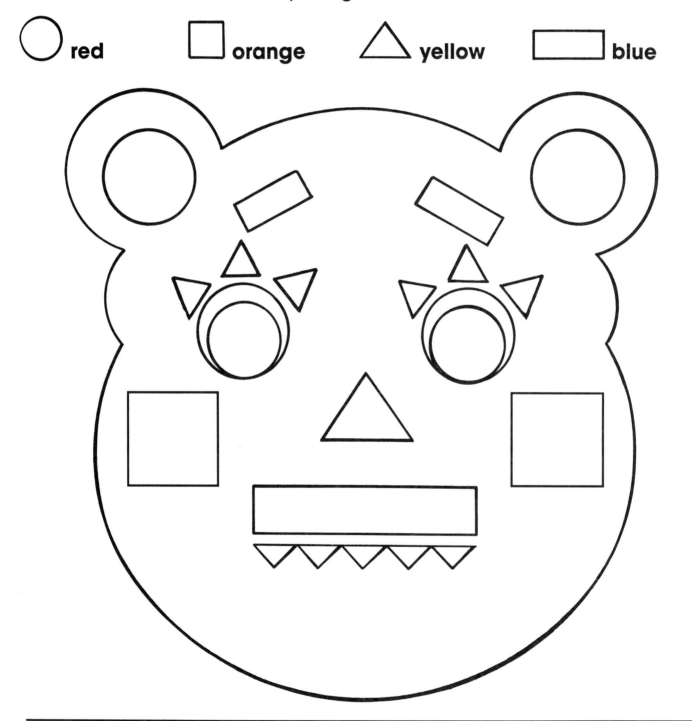

Name _____

Animal Shapes

Color:

squares	——	green
rectangles	——	yellow
circles	——	red
triangles	——	blue

91

MATH

Name _____

"Squaring" Off

Square dancing is a kind of folk dancing. The name of the dance comes from the shape the group of dancers form when they begin the dance – a square. As they dance, they form other shapes.

Look at the shapes and answer the questions.

How many 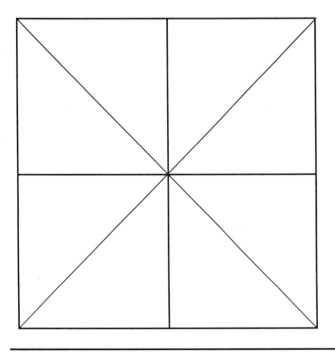's can you find?

_____

One pattern the dancers form is called "a star." Each person puts one arm into the middle of the square. The square is cut into △'s.

How many △'s can you find?

_____

Name _____

Rainbow-Colored Numbers

Color: 1's—red
      2's—blue
      3's—yellow
      4's—green
      5's—orange

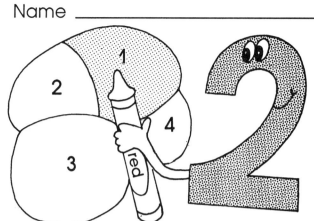

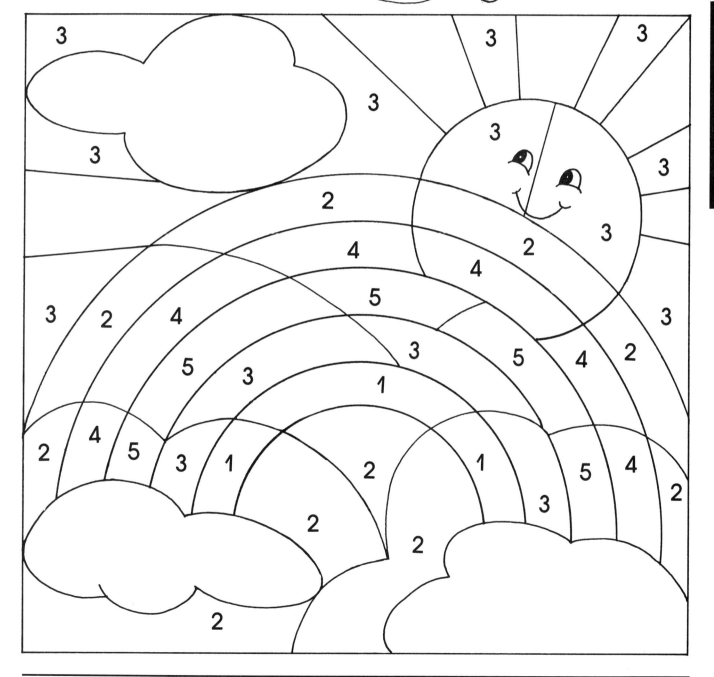

Name _____

One Beautiful Butterfly

Color: 6's—purple
7's—yellow
8's—black
9's—orange
10's—brown

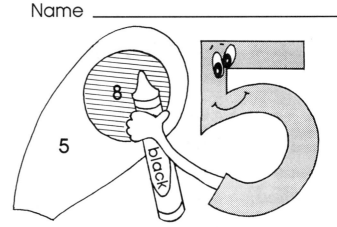

Name _____

Clown Count

the 🎈's:

1 - blue   2 - orange   3 - yellow   4 - green

5 - purple   6 - brown

7 - red   8 - black   9 - blue   10 - purple

Color clown, too!

MATH

Name _____

Wintry Ride

Count each set of bears. Draw a line from each set to the sled that has the correct number.

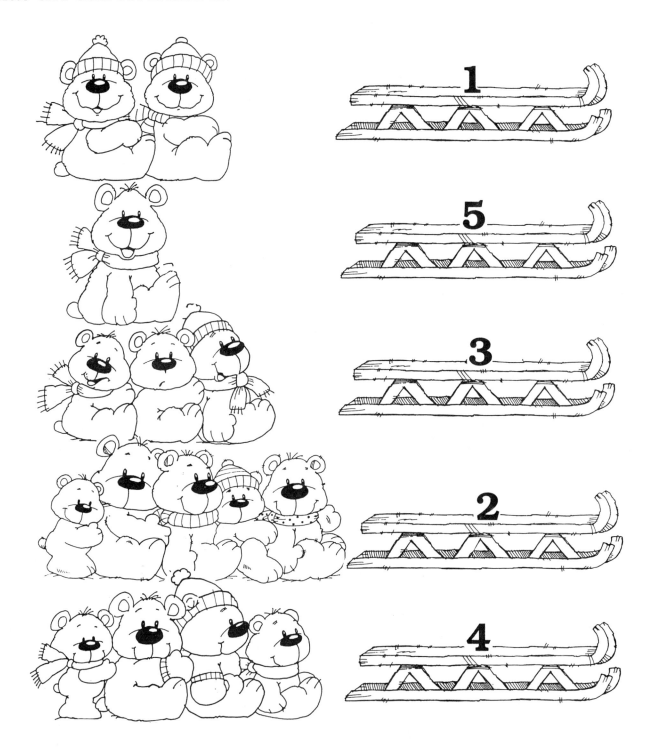

Name _____

Pack a Snack

Count each set of sandwiches. Draw a line from each set to the backpack that has the correct number.

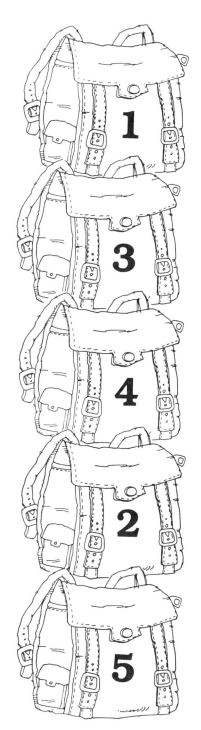

IF8693 Super Book for Grade 1

MATH

Name _____

Sheepish Shepherd

Count the sheep on each hill. Then write that number on each tree.

Name _____

Number Express

Number the train.

Draw a line from the word to the number.

seven	1
two	8
five	3
nine	4
six	7
four	5
one	6
three	2
eight	9

Color train cars. one-**red** three-**green** five-**orange**

two-**blue** four-**yellow** six-**brown**

Name _____

Beach Blanket Numbers
Count. Use code to color answers.

1—blue	4—red	7—purple
2—yellow	5—orange	8—gray
3—green	6—brown	9—black

Name _____

School Scene

How many?

MATH

Name _____

Take an Animal Count!

Count the zoo animals in each box. Match the number to the correct number word by drawing a line to it. One is done for you.

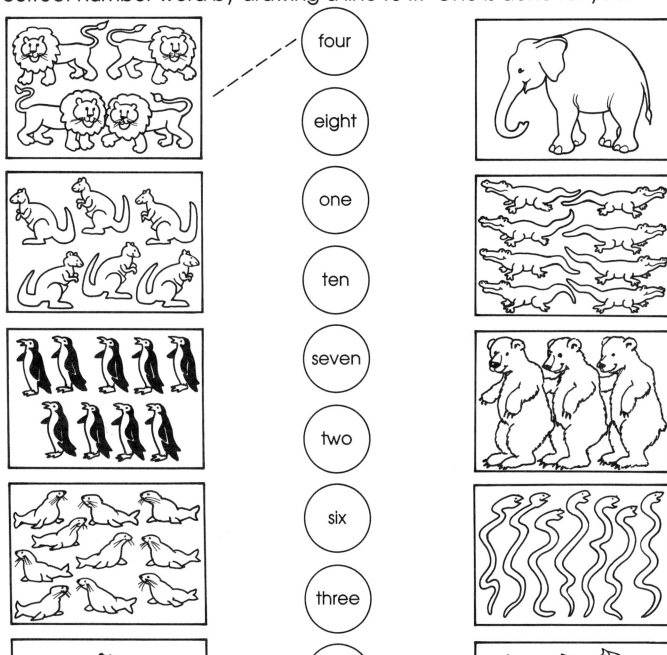

Name _____

Connect the Dots

Join the dots in order.
Color the surprise.

•1

•3

20• /

•2

15•

•4

•16

14•

6•

•5

•19

•7

•8

•17

13•

•18

12•

11•)) •10)) •9

Name _____

More Dot-to-Dot Fun

Connect the dots.

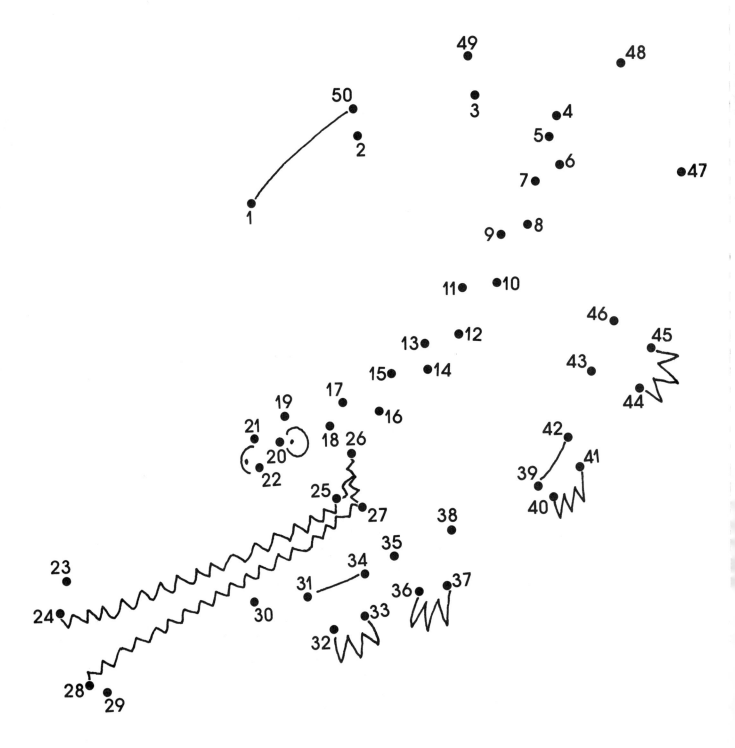

Name _____

Happy Hikers

Hike your way to camp. Trace a path through the maze by counting from 1 to 10 in the correct order. Color the picture.

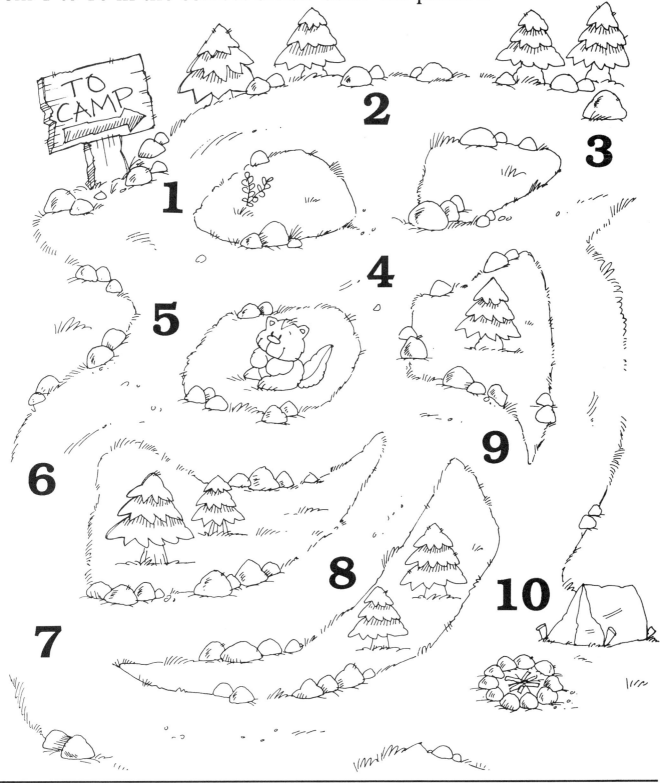

MATH

Name _____

Two for the Pool

Counting by 2's, write the numbers to 50 in the waterdrops. Start at the top of the slide and go down.

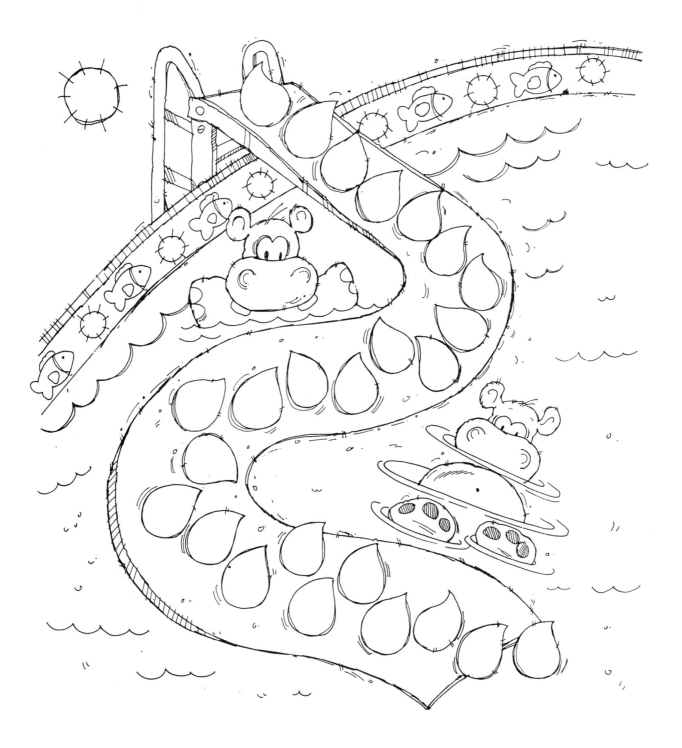

Name _____

I'm Counting on You

Write and count by 2's.

Write and count by 5's.

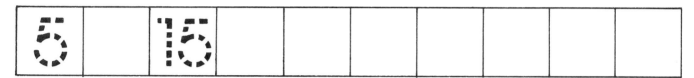

Connect the dots by 2's.

Connect the dots by 5's.

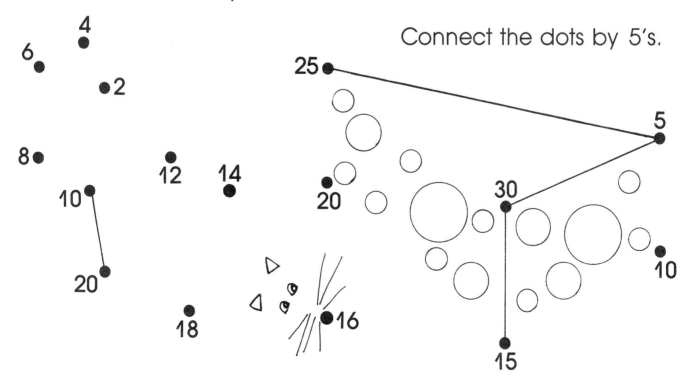

Name _____

Count the Cookie Clues

Find out what holds something crumbly, but good! Counting by 5's, connect the dots in order. Start with 5. Color the picture.

Name _____

Desert Trek

As you count by 10's, color each canteen with the number you say to lead the camel to the watering hole.

IF8693 Super Book for Grade 1

MATH

Name _____

Caterpillar Count

Circle numbers counting by twos.

Count by 2's.

| 1, ②, 3, 4, 5, 6, 7,
8, 9, 10, 11, 12, 13,
14, 15, 16, 17, 18, 19,
20, 21, 22, 23, 24 |

2 , 4 , ____ , ____ , ____ , ____ , ____ , ____

Put △ around numbers counting by fives.

Count by 5's.

| 1, 2, 3, 4, △5, 6, 7, 8, 9,
10, 11, 12, 13, 14, 15, 16,
17, 18, 19, 20, 21, 22,
23, 24, 25, 26, 27,
28, 29, 30, 31, 32, 33,
34, 35, 36, 37, 38, 39, 40 |

5 , 10 , ____ , ____ , ____ , ____ , ____ , ____

Put ☐ around numbers counting by 10's.

Count by 10's.

| 1, 2, 3, 4, 5, 6, 7, 8, 9, 10, 11,
12, 13, 14, 15, 16, 17, 18, 19,
20, 21, 22, 23, 24, 25, 26,
27, 28, 29, 30, 31, 32, 33 |

10 , ____ , ____ , ____ , ____ , ____ , ____ , ____

Name _____

Largest and Smallest

In the shapes, circle the smallest number.

Draw a square around the largest number.

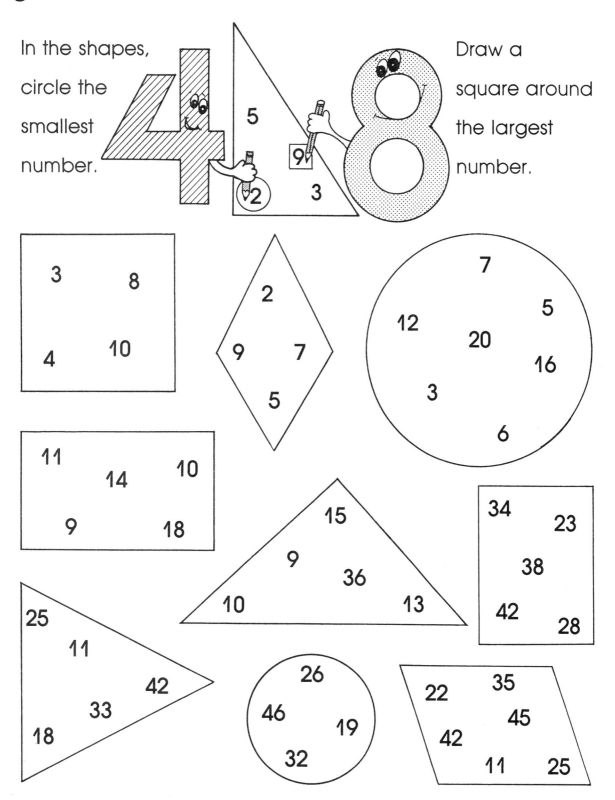

Name _____

Barking Up a Tree

Use counters. Trace or draw each set you make. Then, write how many in all.

How many?   How many more?   How many in all?

| 3 | + | 2 | = | _____ |

| 2 | + | 1 | = | _____ |

| 4 | + | 3 | = | _____ |

| 1 | + | 6 | = | _____ |

Think of a story for this picture. Write how many in all.

_____ in all

       IF8693 Super Book for Grade 1

Name _____

How Many in All?

$2 + 2 = 4$

Write an addition sentence and a vertical fact for each picture story.
Find how many in all.

___
+ ___
___

___ + ___ = ___

___
+ ___
___

___ + ___ = ___

___
+ ___
___

___ + ___ = ___

___
+ ___
___

___ + ___ = ___

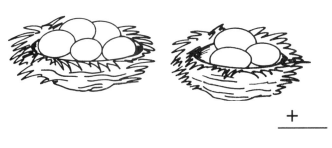

___
+ ___
___

___ + ___ = ___

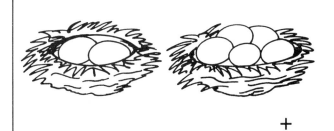

___
+ ___
___

___ + ___ = ___

IF8693 Super Book for Grade 1

MATH

Name _____

Addition Using Counters

| Example | $2 + 1 = \underline{?}$

Use counters to add.

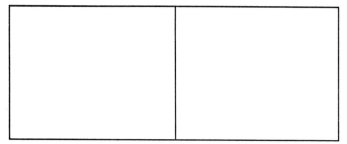

Put in 2.   Put in 1 more.

How many counters are there in all? __3__

So, $2 + 1 = \underline{3}$. The number that tells how many in all is called the **sum**. The sum of 2 + 1 is 3.

Use counters to find each sum.

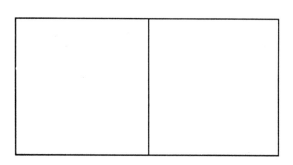

$2 + 4 = \underline{}$

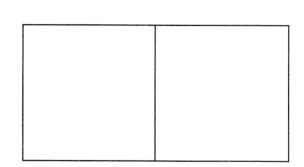

$5 + 2 = \underline{}$

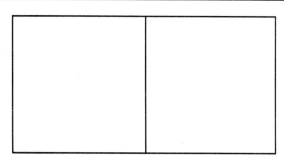

$3 + 3 = \underline{}$

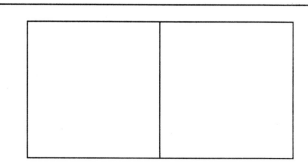

$3 + 4 = \underline{}$

Name _____

Prehistoric Picture Problems

Circle the picture which matches the number sentence.

1. $1 + 2 = 3$

or

2. $2 + 3 = 5$

or

3. $4 + 2 = 6$

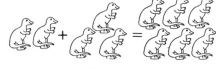

or

4. $5 + 1 = 6$

or

5. $3 + 4 = 7$

or

6. $6 + 1 = 7$

or

Name _____

Alien Problems

Look at the pictures and finish the number sentences.

1.

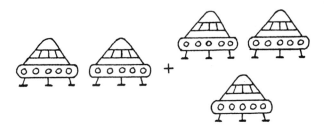

$2 + 3 = \underline{5}$

2.

$1 + 7 = \underline{\hphantom{00}}$

3.

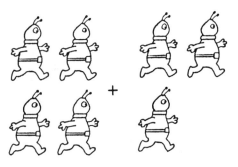

$4 + 3 = \underline{\hphantom{00}}$

4.

$5 + 0 = \underline{\hphantom{00}}$

5.

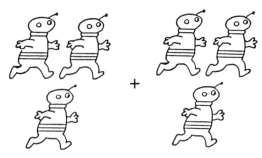

$3 + 3 = \underline{\hphantom{00}}$

6.

$4 + 5 = \underline{\hphantom{00}}$

 IF8693 Super Book for Grade 1

Name _____

Bear Necessities: How Many More Are Needed?

Draw in the missing pictures and finish the number sentences.

1.

$1 + \underline{2} = 3$

2.

$3 + \underline{} = 5$

3.

$5 + \underline{} = 8$

4.

$3 + \underline{} = 6$

5.

$2 + \underline{} = 7$

6.

$4 + \underline{} = 5$

IF8693 Super Book for Grade 1

Name _____

The Missing Chickens

Draw in the missing pictures and finish the number sentences.

1.

___1___ + 2 = 3

2.

_____ + 3 = 6

3.

5 + _____ = 7

4.

_____ + 3 = 5

5.

_____ + 4 = 8

6.

7 + _____ = 8

Name _____

How Many Robots in All?

Look at the pictures and finish the number sentences.

1.

How many 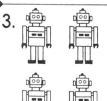's are there in all?

$2 + 4 = $ _____

2.

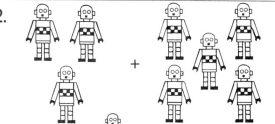

How many 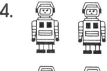's are there in all?

$3 + 5 = $ _____

3.

How many 's are there in all?

$4 + 3 = $ _____

4.

How many 's are there in all?

$4 + 1 = $ _____

5.

How many 's are there in all?

$2 + 5 = $ _____

6.

How many 's are there in all?

$4 + 4 = $ _____

MATH

Name _____

How Many Rabbits?

Look at the pictures and finish the number sentences.

1.

How many 's are there in all?

$1 + 1 = \underline{2}$

2.

How many 's are there in all?

$3 + 6 = \underline{}$

3.

How many 's are there in all?

$6 + 1 = \underline{}$

4.

How many 's are there in all?

$3 + 4 = \underline{}$

5.

How many 's are there in all?

$4 + 5 = \underline{}$

6.

How many 's are there in all?

$2 + 3 = \underline{}$

IF8693 Super Book for Grade 1

Name _____

Bee Addition

 +   3 + 1 =

Add. Use code to color each bee.

2—red	4—blue
3—yellow	5—green

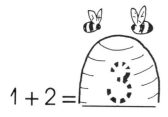

1 + 2 = ____

2 + 3 = ____

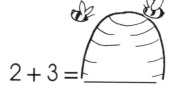

3 + 2 = ____

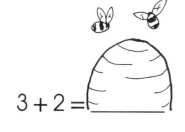

3 + 1 = ____

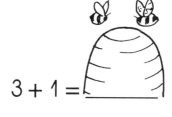

1 + 1 = ____

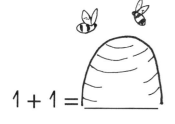

2 + 2 = ____

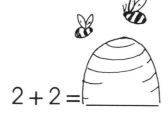

2 + 1 = ____

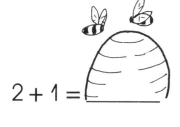

1 + 3 = ____

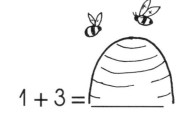

MATH

Name _____

Lumberjack Facts

Add.

If the answer equals **1**, color the space **red**.
If the answer equals **2**, color the space **yellow**.
If the answer equals **3**, color the space **black**.
If the answer equals **4**, color the space **blue**.
If the answer equals **5**, color the space **brown**.
If the answer equals **6**, color the space **green**.

Name _____

Creature Count

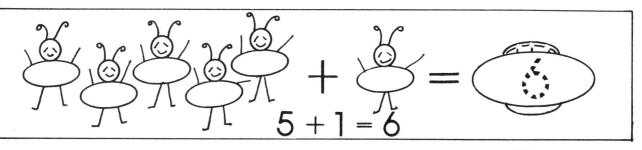

$5 + 1 = 6$

$4 + 6 =$ $1 + 9 =$

$7 + 1 =$ $7 + 3 =$

$5 + 2 =$ $6 + 1 =$

$8 + 2 =$ $3 + 5 =$

$6 + 3 =$ $6 + 2 =$

$4 + 5 =$  $1 + 7 =$

IF8693 Super Book for Grade 1

Name _____

Beary Good

Put counters on each bear to show the addition. Write the sums.

3 + 2 = ___   5 + 0 = ___   1 + 6 = ___   4 + 2 = ___

$$
\begin{array}{cc} 6 \\ + 1 \\ \hline \end{array}
\qquad
\begin{array}{cc} 3 \\ + 4 \\ \hline \end{array}
\qquad
\begin{array}{cc} 2 \\ + 3 \\ \hline \end{array}
\qquad
\begin{array}{cc} 5 \\ + 2 \\ \hline \end{array}
\qquad
\begin{array}{cc} 7 \\ + 1 \\ \hline \end{array}
\qquad
\begin{array}{cc} 0 \\ + 2 \\ \hline \end{array}
$$

$$
\begin{array}{cc} 8 \\ + 0 \\ \hline \end{array}
\qquad
\begin{array}{cc} 4 \\ + 5 \\ \hline \end{array}
\qquad
\begin{array}{cc} 3 \\ + 6 \\ \hline \end{array}
\qquad
\begin{array}{cc} 2 \\ + 6 \\ \hline \end{array}
\qquad
\begin{array}{cc} 3 \\ + 5 \\ \hline \end{array}
\qquad
\begin{array}{cc} 6 \\ + 2 \\ \hline \end{array}
$$

Name _____

Animal Addition

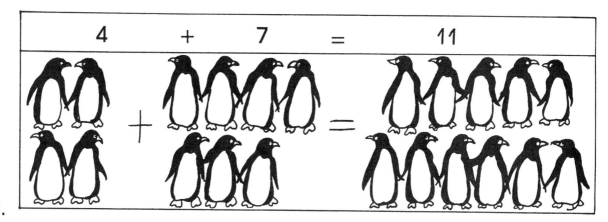

| 4 | + | 7 | = | 11 |

Add.

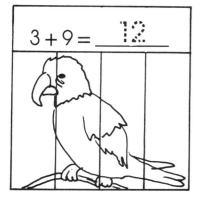

3 + 9 = __12__

6 + 7 = _____

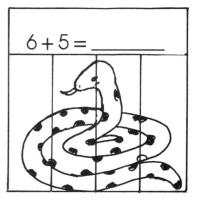

6 + 5 = _____

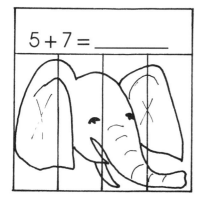

5 + 7 = _____

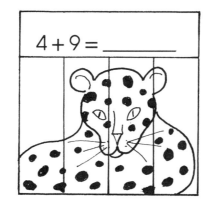

4 + 9 = _____

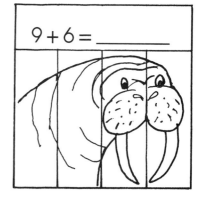

9 + 6 = _____

7 + 7 = _____

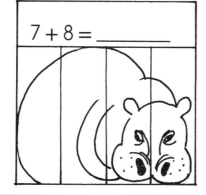

7 + 8 = _____

6 + 8 = _____

IF8693 Super Book for Grade 1

MATH

Name _____

Add the Apples

Match.

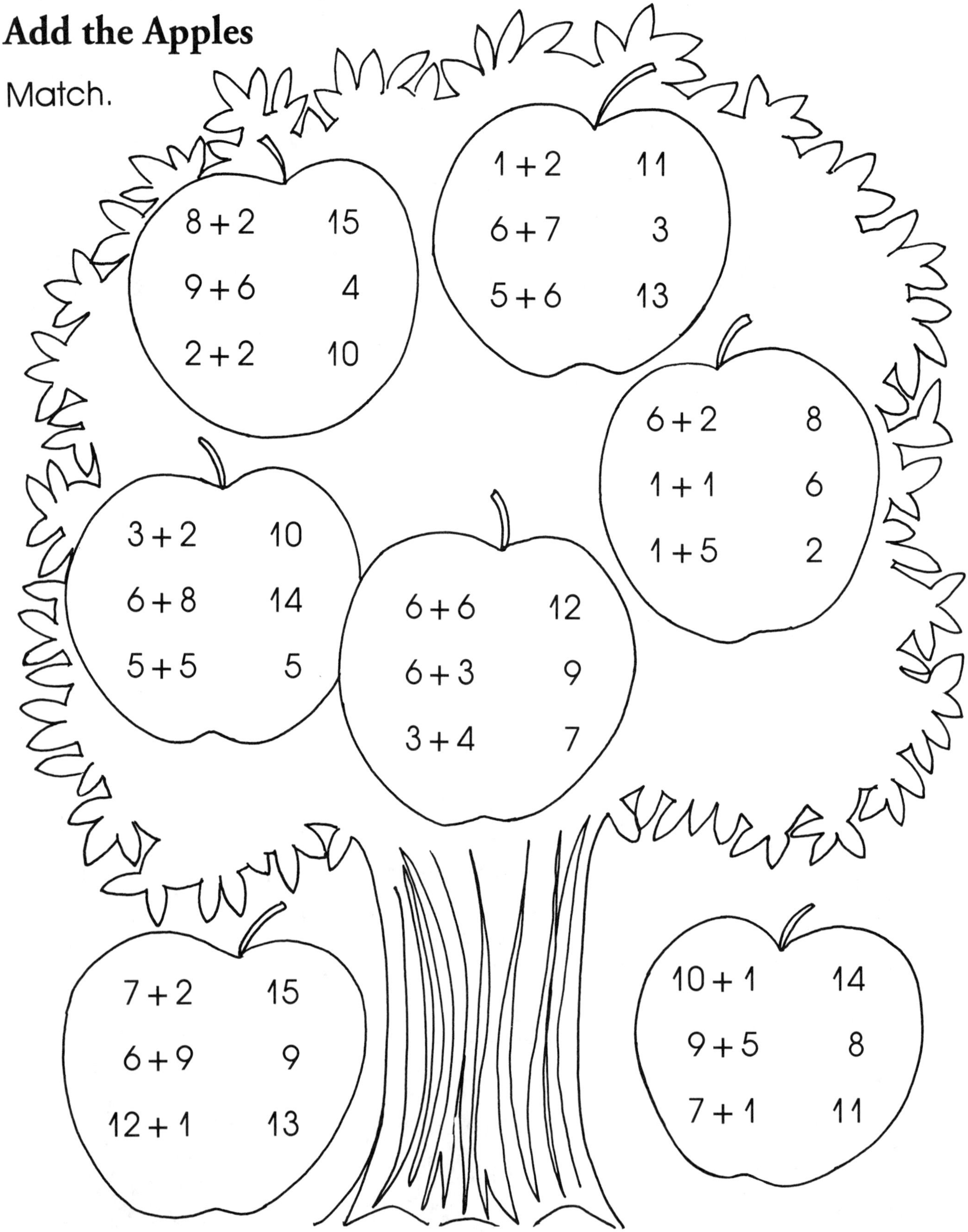

8 + 2   15

9 + 6   4

2 + 2   10

1 + 2   11

6 + 7   3

5 + 6   13

6 + 2   8

1 + 1   6

1 + 5   2

3 + 2   10

6 + 8   14

5 + 5   5

6 + 6   12

6 + 3   9

3 + 4   7

7 + 2   15

6 + 9   9

12 + 1   13

10 + 1   14

9 + 5   8

7 + 1   11

Name _____

What's the Difference?

| Example | $5 - 2 = \underline{?}$ |

Use counters to subtract.

Put in 5. Take away 2.

How many counters are left? _3_

So, $5 - 2 = 3$. The number that tells how many are left is called the **difference**. The difference of $5 - 2$ is 3.

Use counters to find each difference.

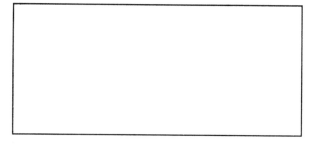

$6 - 3 = \underline{}$

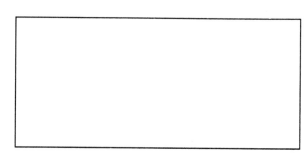

$5 - 1 = \underline{}$

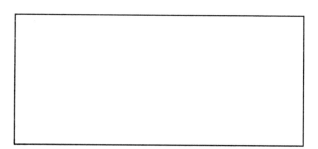

$5 - 3 = \underline{}$

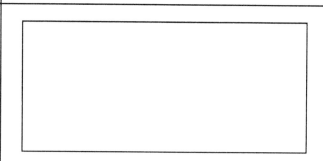

$4 - 2 = \underline{}$

 IF8693 Super Book for Grade 1

Name _____

Counting Kittens

Use counters. Make a set, then take away. Write how many are left.

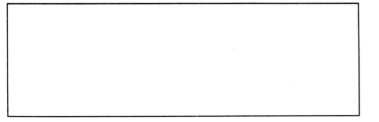

_____
are left.

Put in 4. Take away 1.

_____
are left.

Put in 5. Take away 2.

_____
are left.

Put in 6. Take away 1.

_____
are left.

Put in 7. Take away 3.

Think of a story for this picture. Write how many are left.

_____
are left.

IF8693 Super Book for Grade 1

Name _____

Transportation Problems

Circle the picture which matches the number sentence. Then finish the number sentence.

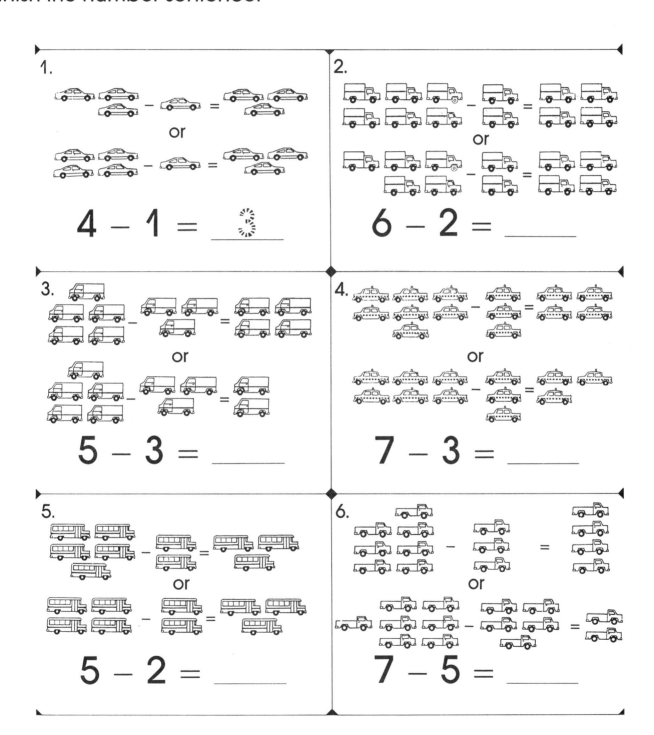

1.

$$4 - 1 = \underline{}$$

2.

$$6 - 2 = \underline{}$$

3.

$$5 - 3 = \underline{}$$

4.

$$7 - 3 = \underline{}$$

5.

$$5 - 2 = \underline{}$$

6.

$$7 - 5 = \underline{}$$

Name _____

Sea Creature Subtraction

Look at the pictures and finish the number sentences.

1.
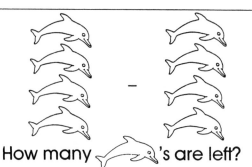
How many 's are left?

$$4 - 4 = 0$$

2.

How many 's are left?

$$6 - 2 = \underline{\quad}$$

3.
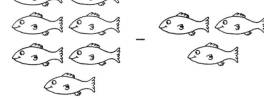
How many 's are left?

$$7 - 3 = \underline{\quad}$$

4.

How many 's are left?

$$6 - 5 = \underline{\quad}$$

5.
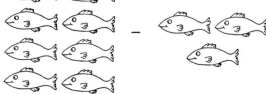
How many 's are left?

$$8 - 3 = \underline{\quad}$$

6.
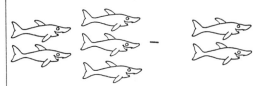
How many 's are left?

$$5 - 2 = \underline{\quad}$$

IF8693 Super Book for Grade 1

Name _____

Nutty Subtraction

Count the nuts.
Write answer on blank.
Circle problems with same answer.

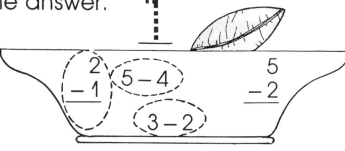

$$\begin{array}{c}2\\-1\end{array}$$ $5-4$ $\begin{array}{c}5\\-2\end{array}$

$3-2$

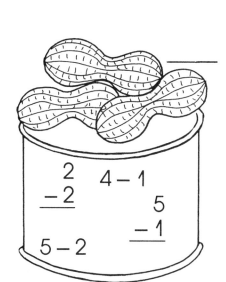

$$\begin{array}{c}2\\-2\end{array}\quad 4-1$$

$$\begin{array}{c}5\\-1\end{array}$$

$$5-2$$

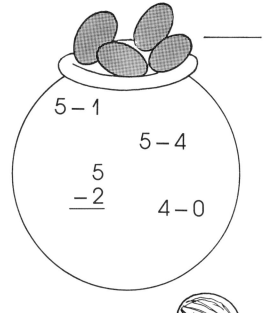

$$5-1$$

$$5-4$$

$$\begin{array}{c}5\\-2\end{array}$$

$$4-0$$

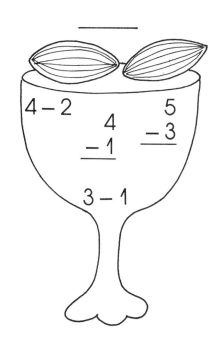

$$4-2\qquad \begin{array}{c}5\\-3\end{array}$$

$$\begin{array}{c}4\\-1\end{array}$$

$$3-1$$

$$5-0\qquad \begin{array}{c}2\\-2\end{array}$$

$$\begin{array}{c}5\\-1\end{array}\quad \begin{array}{c}4\\-3\end{array}$$

Name _____

Robins and Worms

$$3 - 2 = 1$$

$$\begin{array}{r} 3 \\ -2 \\ \hline 1 \end{array}$$

5 – 1 = _____   3 – 1 = _____   5 – 2 = _____

4 – 1 = _____   2 – 1 = _____   4 – 2 = _____

3 – 2 = _____   4 – 3 = _____   5 – 3 = _____

Subtract. Use code to color worms.   **1—red   3—yellow**
2—orange   4—brown

5 – 1 = ◯   4 – 2 = ◯   5 – 2 = ◯

$$\begin{array}{r} 5 \\ -1 \\ \hline \end{array}$$ $$\begin{array}{r} 4 \\ -2 \\ \hline \end{array}$$ $$\begin{array}{r} 5 \\ -2 \\ \hline \end{array}$$

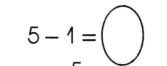

3 – 1 = ◯   4 – 3 = ◯   5 – 3 = ◯

$$\begin{array}{r} 3 \\ -1 \\ \hline \end{array}$$ $$\begin{array}{r} 4 \\ -3 \\ \hline \end{array}$$ $$\begin{array}{r} 5 \\ -3 \\ \hline \end{array}$$

 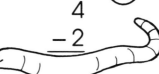 

2 – 1 = ◯   4 – 1 = ◯   3 – 2 = ◯

$$\begin{array}{r} 2 \\ -1 \\ \hline \end{array}$$ $$\begin{array}{r} 4 \\ -1 \\ \hline \end{array}$$ $$\begin{array}{r} 3 \\ -2 \\ \hline \end{array}$$

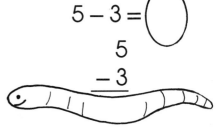 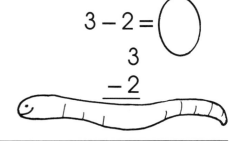

       IF8693 Super Book for Grade 1

Name _____

"Berry" Tasty

Subtract.

If the answer is **0**, color the space **green**.

If the answer is **1**, color the space **brown**.

If the answer is **2**, color the space **blue**.

If the answer is **3**, color the space **purple**.

If the answer is **4**, color the space **black**.

If the answer is **5**, color the space **pink**.

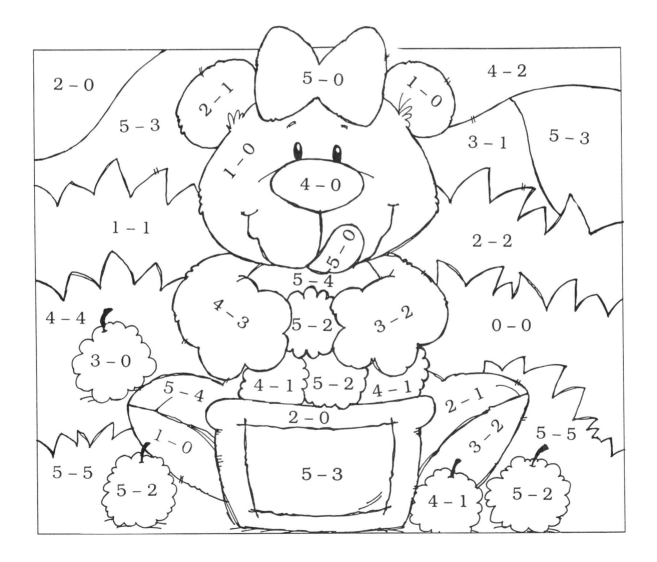

Name _____

Bubbly Baths

Subtract. Write each answer on the rubber duck.

5 – 4

1 – 0

4 – 2

2 – 1

3 – 1

3 – 2

4 – 1

1 – 1

5 – 1

5 – 2

Name _____

Fewer Fruits

$$9 - 2 = 7$$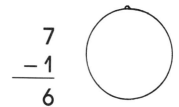

$$\begin{array}{r} 7 \\ -\ 1 \\ \hline 6 \end{array}$$

Subtract. Use code to color.

6—orange   9—green
7—red   10—purple
8—yellow

$11 - 1 =$ 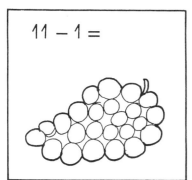	$\begin{array}{r} 9 \\ -\ 1 \end{array}$ 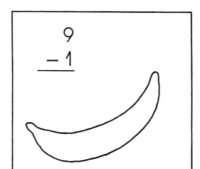	$8 - 1 =$ 
$10 - 4 =$ 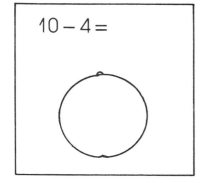	$\begin{array}{r} 9 \\ -\ 2 \end{array}$ 	$\begin{array}{r} 10 \\ -\ 1 \end{array}$ 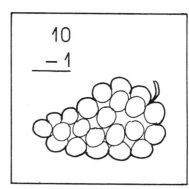
$10 - 2 =$ 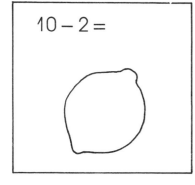	$11 - 2 =$ 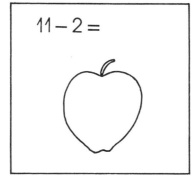	$\begin{array}{r} 10 \\ -\ 3 \end{array}$ 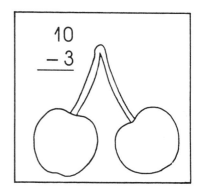

MATH

Name _____

Sweet Treats

Count the candy.
Write number on blank.
Circle problems with same answer.

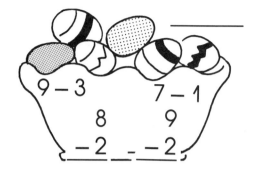

$9 - 3$ $7 - 1$

$$\begin{array}{r} 8 \\ -2 \end{array}$$ $$\begin{array}{r} 9 \\ -2 \end{array}$$

$10 - 1$

$10 - 4$

$$\begin{array}{r} 11 \\ -2 \end{array}$$ $$\begin{array}{r} 9 \\ -1 \end{array}$$

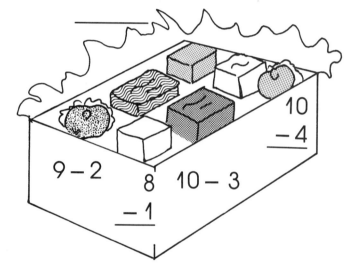

$$\begin{array}{r} 10 \\ -4 \end{array}$$

$9 - 2$ $$\begin{array}{r} 8 \\ -1 \end{array}$$ $10 - 3$

$$\begin{array}{r} 10 \\ -4 \end{array}$$ $7 - 2$ $$\begin{array}{r} 8 \\ -2 \end{array}$$

$8 - 2$

$$\begin{array}{r} 9 \\ -4 \end{array}$$ $10 - 1$ $10 - 2$

$$\begin{array}{r} 9 \\ -1 \end{array}$$

Name _____

A Whale of a Job!

For each problem, put the number of counters needed in the water, then take away by sliding the numbers into the whale's mouth. Then, count how many counters are left in the water to find the difference.

$$
\begin{array}{r} 7 \\ -\ 3 \\ \hline \end{array}
\qquad
\begin{array}{r} 9 \\ -\ 2 \\ \hline \end{array}
\qquad
\begin{array}{r} 6 \\ -\ 4 \\ \hline \end{array}
\qquad
\begin{array}{r} 5 \\ -\ 2 \\ \hline \end{array}
\qquad
\begin{array}{r} 8 \\ -\ 3 \\ \hline \end{array}
$$

$$
\begin{array}{r} 9 \\ -\ 3 \\ \hline \end{array}
\qquad
\begin{array}{r} 6 \\ -\ 3 \\ \hline \end{array}
\qquad
\begin{array}{r} 7 \\ -\ 5 \\ \hline \end{array}
\qquad
\begin{array}{r} 8 \\ -\ 2 \\ \hline \end{array}
\qquad
\begin{array}{r} 5 \\ -\ 1 \\ \hline \end{array}
$$

8 – 4 = _____   6 – 2 = _____   7 – 4 = _____

           IF8693 Super Book for Grade 1

Name _____

Hop Along Numbers

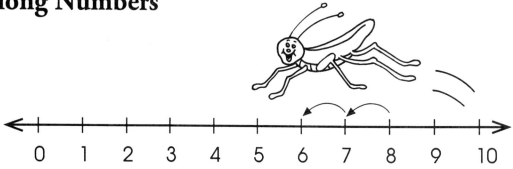

Use the number line to **count back**.

8, _7_ , _6_   6, ___ , ___

5, ___ , ___   7, ___ , ___ , ___

Use the number line to count back to find each difference.

Example: $9 - 2 =$ _?_   Start with 9. Count back 2.

9, ___ , ___ $9 - 2 =$ ___

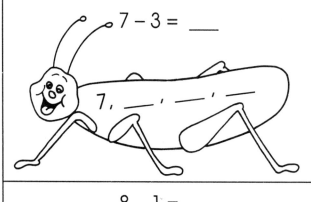

$7 - 3 =$ ___

7, ___ , ___ , ___

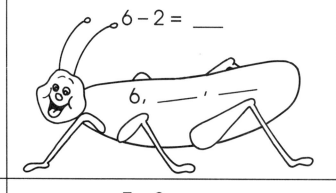

$6 - 2 =$ ___

6, ___ , ___

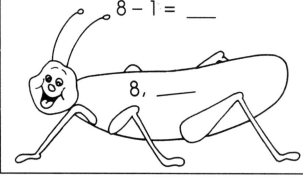

$8 - 1 =$ ___

8, ___

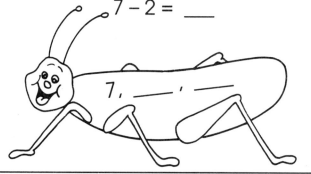

$7 - 2 =$ ___

7, ___ , ___

                                       IF8693 Super Book for Grade 1

Name _____

Crayon Count

Count crayons. Write number on blank.
Circle problems that name answer.

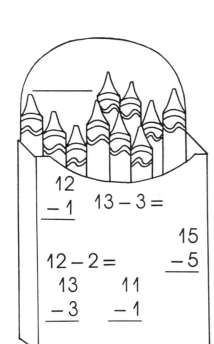

12
− 1   13 − 3 =

                    15
12 − 2 =   − 5
13   11
− 3   − 1

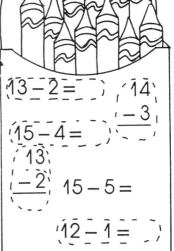

13 − 2 =   14
              − 3
15 − 4 =
13
− 2   15 − 5 =

12 − 1 =

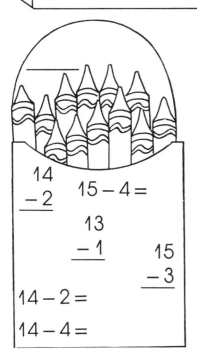

14
− 2   15 − 4 =
13
− 1   15
                − 3
14 − 2 =
14 − 4 =

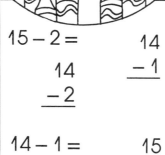

15 − 2 =   14
              − 1
14
− 2
14 − 1 =   15
15 − 3 =   − 2

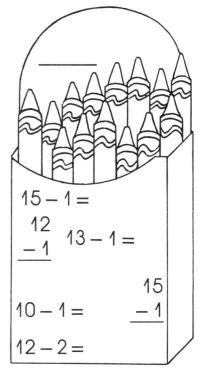

15 − 1 =
12
− 1   13 − 1 =
                    15
10 − 1 =   − 1
12 − 2 =

139   IF8693 Super Book for Grade 1

Name _____

Turtle Math—Take It Slow

Color answer:

2—red
3—blue
4—yellow
5—green

2 + 3

1 + 4

3 − 1

5 − 2

5 − 3

3 + 1

4 + 1

5 − 1

5 − 2

3 + 2

1 + 1

4 − 1

1 + 1

5 − 1

4 − 1

1 + 3

2 + 1

3 + 2

5 − 1

2 + 1

4 − 1

3 − 1

4 − 2

3 + 1

2 + 3

4 − 1

4 + 1

2 + 1

Name _____

It's Show Time

It's time for Packy and Dermit to perform. Look at the problems.

Write **+** or **−** on each peanut to make the problem correct. Then trace a path from peanut to peanut, connecting each elephant to the correct stool. For Packy, connect all of the **+** problems. For Dermit, connect all of the **−** problems.

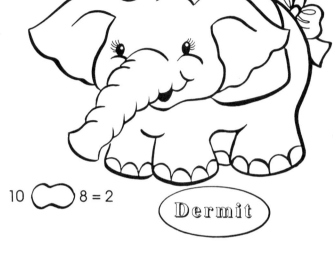

$3 \bigcirc 2 = 5$

$10 \bigcirc 8 = 2$

$2 \bigcirc 6 = 8$

$8 \bigcirc 2 = 6$

$7 \bigcirc 3 = 4$

$5 \bigcirc 4 = 9$

$9 \bigcirc 4 = 5$

$5 \bigcirc 5 = 10$

$3 \bigcirc 3 = 0$

$10 \bigcirc 3 = 7$

$9 \bigcirc 1 = 10$

$7 \bigcirc 5 = 2$

$6 \bigcirc 4 = 10$

$6 \bigcirc 3 = 3$

$5 \bigcirc 2 = 7$

$5 \bigcirc 3 = 8$

$2 \bigcirc 7 = 9$

Name _____

Puppy Problems

Look at the pictures and finish the number sentences.

1.

$5 \oplus 6 = $ __11__

2.

$11 \bigcirc 4 = $ _____

3.

$12 \bigcirc 7 = $ _____

4.

$7 \bigcirc 6 = $ _____

5.

$5 \bigcirc 5 = $ _____

6.

$8 \bigcirc 6 = $ _____

 IF8693 Super Book for Grade 1

Name _____

Calling All Cats

Look at the pictures and finish the number sentences.

1.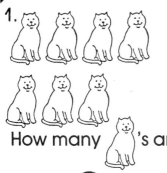

How many 's are there in all?

$7 \oplus 4 = \underline{11}$

2.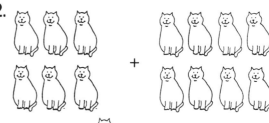

How many 's are there in all?

$6 \bigcirc 8 = \underline{\hphantom{00}}$

3. +

How many 's are there in all?

$11 \bigcirc 2 = \underline{\hphantom{00}}$

4.

How many 's are left?

$13 \bigcirc 7 = \underline{\hphantom{00}}$

5.  –

How many 's are left?

$9 \bigcirc 6 = \underline{\hphantom{00}}$

6.

How many 's are left?

$12 \bigcirc 8 = \underline{\hphantom{00}}$

MATH

Name _____

What Was the Question?

Draw a line under the question that matches the picture. Then finish the number sentence.

1.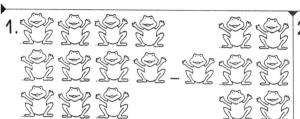

How many 's are there in all?
How many 's are left?

$11 - 7 = \underline{4}$

2.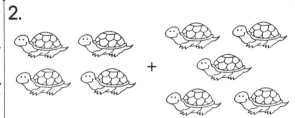

How many 🐢's are there in all?
How many 🐢's are left?

$4 + 5 = \underline{\hspace{1cm}}$

3.

How many 🍄's are there in all?
How many 🍄's are left?

$8 - 3 = \underline{\hspace{1cm}}$

4.

How many 🍄's are there in all?
How many 🍄's are left?

$10 - 4 = \underline{\hspace{1cm}}$

5.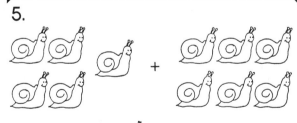

How many 🐌's are there in all?
How many 🐌's are left?

$5 + 6 = \underline{\hspace{1cm}}$

6.

How many 🐸's are there in all?
How many 🐸's are left?

$8 + 4 = \underline{\hspace{1cm}}$

Name _____

Sunny Day Delight

Draw a line under the question that matches the picture.
Then finish the number sentence.

1.
 +

How many 's are there in all?
How many 's are left?

$6 + 6 =$ _12_

2.
 −

How many 's are there in all?
How many 's are left?

$13 - 4 =$ _____

3.
+

How many 's are there in all?
How many 's are left?

$9 + 5 =$ _____

4.
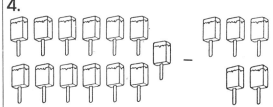 −

How many 's are there in all?
How many 's are left?

$13 - 5 =$ _____

5.
 +

How many 's are there in all?
How many 's are left?

$7 + 7 =$ _____

6.
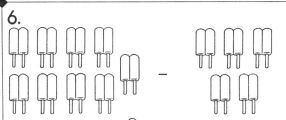 −

How many 's are there in all?
How many 's are left?

$9 - 5 =$ _____

Name _____

Fishing for Answers

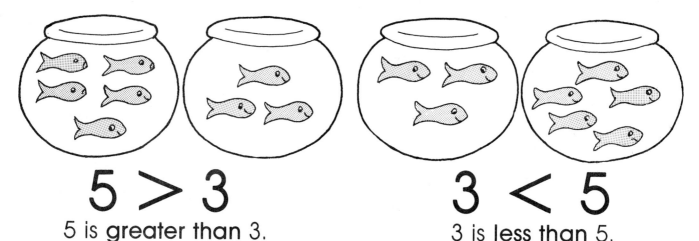

$5 > 3$

5 is **greater than** 3.

$3 < 5$

3 is **less than** 5.

Fill in number line.

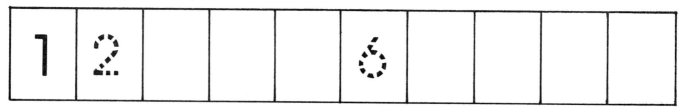

1	2				6				

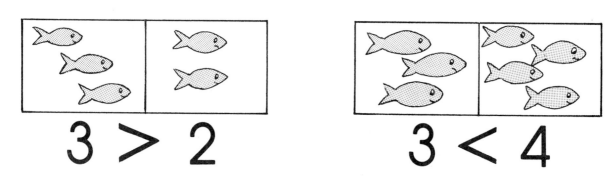

$3 > 2$

$3 < 4$

Write $>$ or $<$. Use number line to help you.

5 _____ 2   1 _____ 7   1 _____ 9   8 _____ 5

3 _____ 4   9 _____ 3   8 _____ 7   2 _____ 4

6 _____ 5   5 _____ 3   5 _____ 7   3 _____ 5

7 _____ 3   7 _____ 6   2 _____ 8   4 _____ 2

         IF8693 Super Book for Grade 1

Name _____

Split in Two

How many equal parts? 2

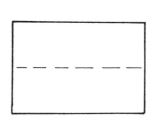

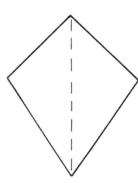

Color shapes with 2 equal parts.

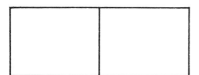

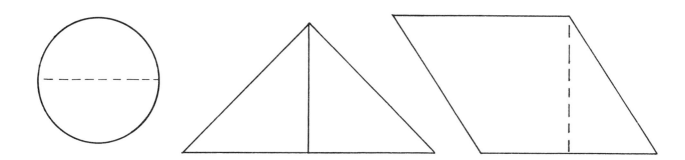

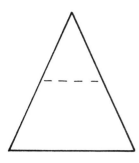

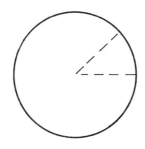

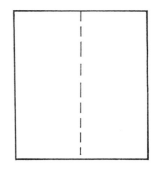

Name _____

Thirds

How many equal parts? __3__

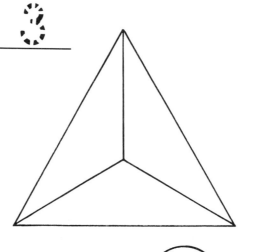

Color shapes with 3 equal parts.

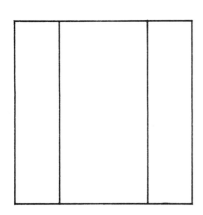

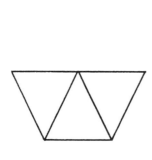

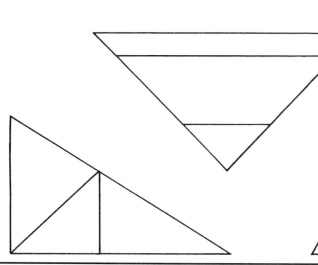

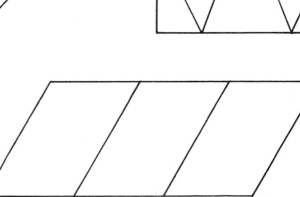

Name _____

Fourths

How many equal parts? ___4___

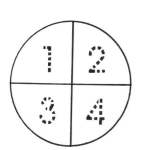  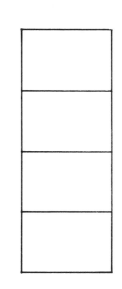

Color shapes with 4 equal parts.

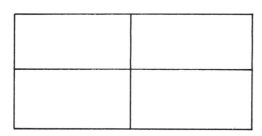 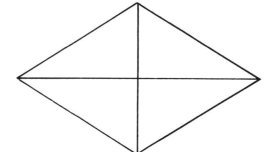

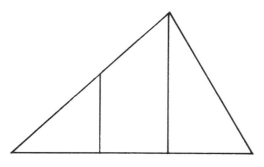 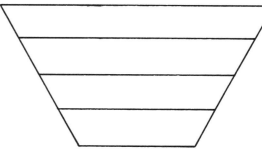

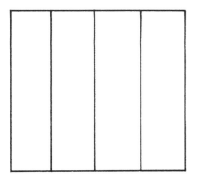 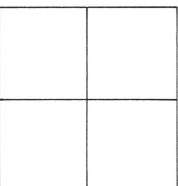 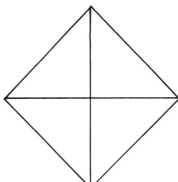

 IF8693 Super Book for Grade 1

Name _____

Fractions Review

How many equal parts?

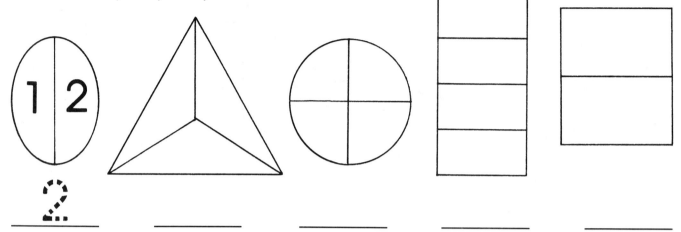

Color shapes with 2 equal parts red,
3 parts blue and 4 parts green.

Name _____

A Race!

first
second
third
fourth
fifth
sixth
seventh

Write the correct word to tell where each runner placed in the race.

1. _____

2. _____

3. _____

4. _____

5. _____

6. _____

7. _____

Flip Fun! Draw a prize you would like to receive for winning a race.

MATH

Name _____

Flags First

Color the **ninth** flag red.
Write **O** on the **second** flag.
Color the **eighth** flag blue.
Write **D** on the **fourth** flag.
Color the **sixth** flag yellow.
Write **G** on the **first** flag.
Color the **tenth** flag purple.
Write **O** on the **third** flag.
Color the **seventh** flag green.
Color the **fifth** flag orange.

Name _____

Balls of All Kinds

Color second
ball brown.

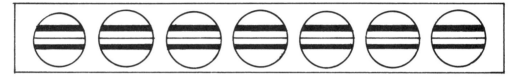

Color sixth
ball yellow.

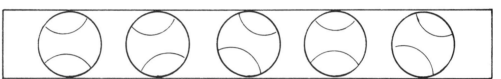

Color fourth
ball orange.

Color first
ball black.

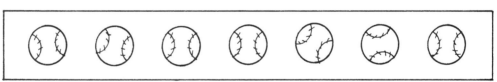

Color third
ball blue.

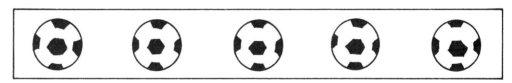

Color fifth
ball green.

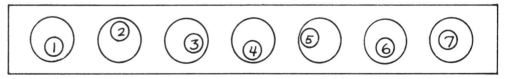

Color seventh
ball purple.

Color eighth
ball pink.

MATH

Name _____

Henny Penny

(1¢) 1 penny
1 cent

How much money?
Example

(1¢)(1¢)(1¢)
(1¢)(1¢)=[5]¢

(1¢)(1¢)(1¢)(1¢)
(1¢)(1¢)=☐¢

(1¢)(1¢)=☐¢

(1¢)(1¢)(1¢)=☐¢

(1¢)(1¢)(1¢)
(1¢)=☐¢

(1¢)(1¢)(1¢)(1¢)
(1¢)(1¢)(1¢)(1¢)=☐¢

(1¢)(1¢)(1¢)(1¢)(1¢)(1¢)(1¢)=☐¢

Name _____

Penny Pinchers

Draw a line from the pennies to the
right numbers.

Example

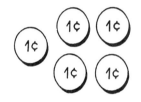

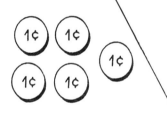

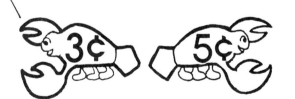

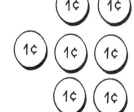

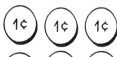

     IF8693 Super Book for Grade 1

Name _____

Nickel Pickles

 5 cents
1 nickel

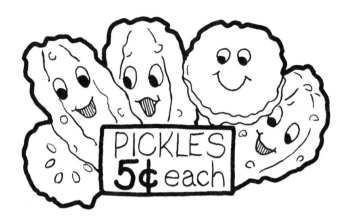

How much money?

 = 15 ¢

Count 5 , 10 , 15

 = ☐ ¢

Count___, ___

 = ☐ ¢

Count___, ___, ___

___, ___

 = ☐ ¢

Count___, ___, ___

___, ___

(5¢)(5¢)/(5¢)(5¢) = ☐ ¢

Count___, ___, ___, ___

(5¢)(5¢)(5¢)/(5¢)(5¢)(5¢) = ☐ ¢

Count___, ___, ___

___, ___, ___

Name _____

Five Hive

How much money is in each hive?

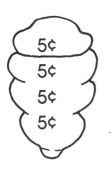 __20__ ¢

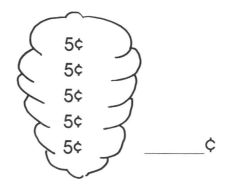 _____ ¢

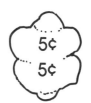 _____ ¢

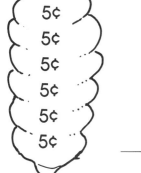 _____ ¢

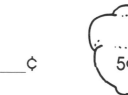 _____ ¢

 _____ ¢

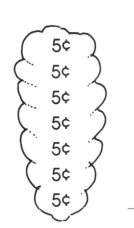 _____ ¢

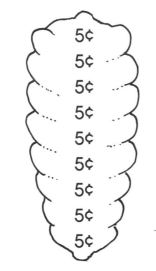 _____ ¢

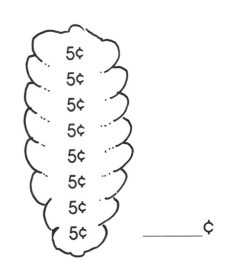 _____ ¢

IF8693 Super Book for Grade 1

Name _____

Money Bunnies

Count the coins. Write the amount under each bunny's carrot.

Name _____

Cent-erpillars

Count the coins on each "cent"erpillar.

_**17**_ ¢

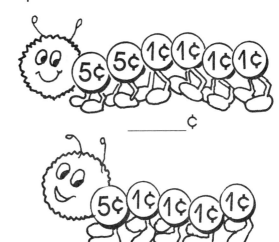

_____ ¢

_____ ¢

_____ ¢

_____ ¢

_____ ¢

_____ ¢

_____ ¢

_____ ¢

_____ ¢

IF8693 Super Book for Grade 1

MATH

Name _____

Marching Dimes

Come march with my dime friends and me!

Count by 10's.

____10__ ¢   _____   _____

_____   _____   _____

Count by 10's. Write the number. Make a circle around the group which is **more**.

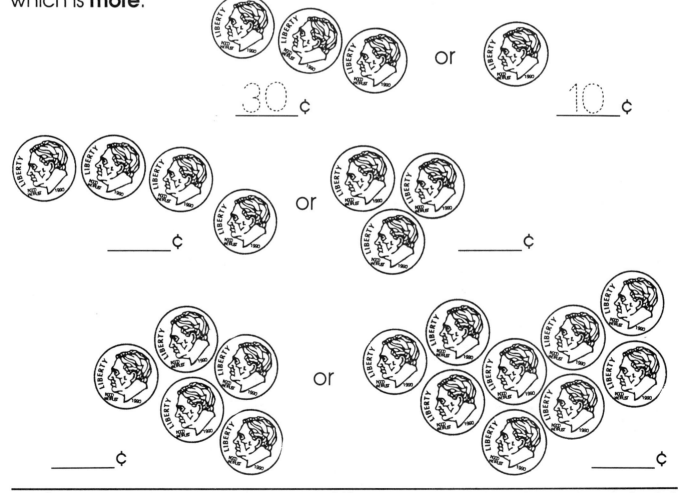

___30__ ¢   ___10__ ¢

_____ ¢   _____ ¢

_____ ¢   _____ ¢

       IF8693 Super Book for Grade 1

Name _____

Dime Climbs

Climb the trees and count the money.
Write the answer under each tree.

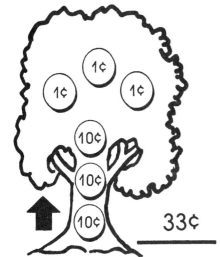

33¢

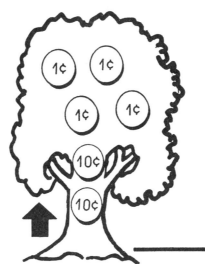

_____

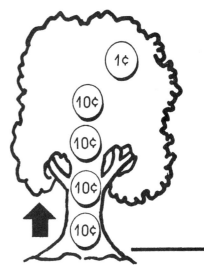

_____

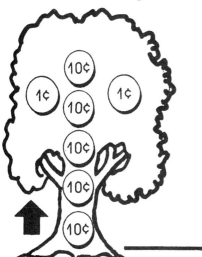

_____

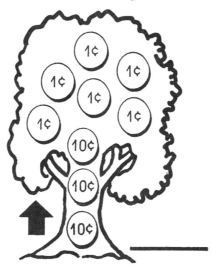

_____

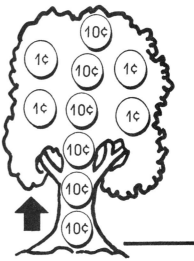

_____

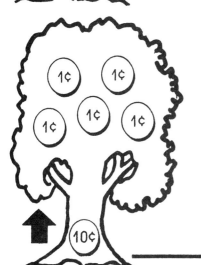

_____

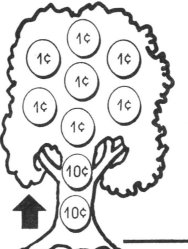

_____

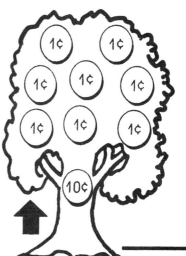

_____

MATH

Name _____

Buy and Buy

Circle the coins to equal the right amount.

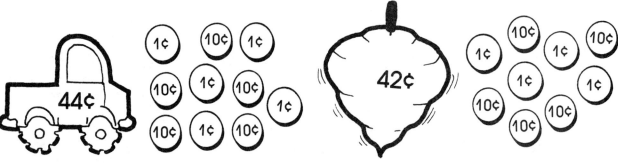

IF8693 Super Book for Grade 1

Sir Circle Counts Coins!

Name _____

Count the coins. Circle the set with more money.

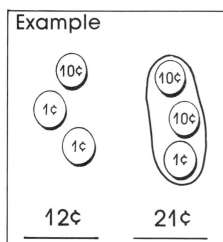

Example

12¢ ___   21¢ ___

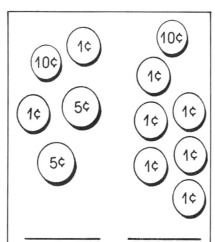

___   ___

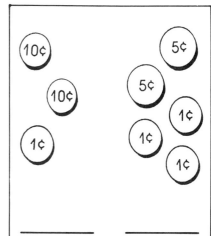

___   ___

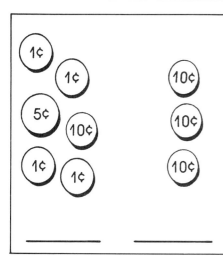

___   ___

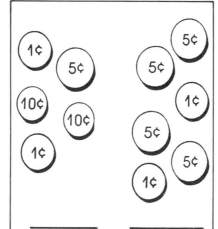

___   ___

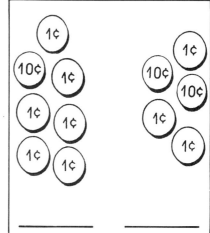

___   ___

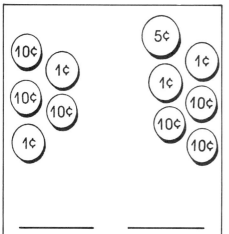

___   ___

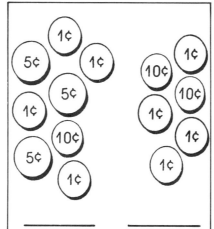

___   ___

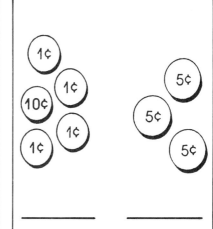

___   ___

IF8693 Super Book for Grade 1

MATH

Name _____

Watch the Time

Show the class how to put numbers on the watch and draw watch hands. Students then color and cut out the watch. Tape it to fit the wrist.

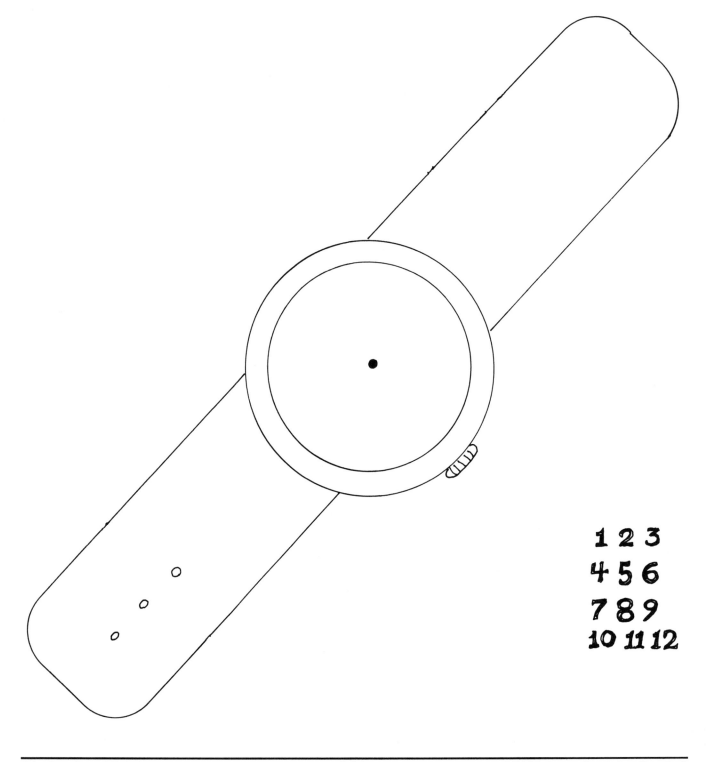

1 2 3
4 5 6
7 8 9
10 11 12

Name _____

Hickory Dickory Dock

What time is it?

___o'clock

___o'clock

___o'clock

___o'clock

___o'clock

___o'clock

___o'clock

___o'clock

___o'clock

___o'clock

___o'clock

___o'clock

MATH

IF8693 Super Book for Grade 1

Name _____

Here's the Scoop!

Draw the hour hand on each clock.

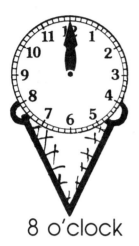

8 o'clock

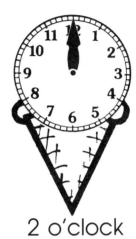

4 o'clock

2 o'clock

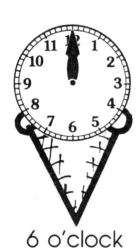

6 o'clock

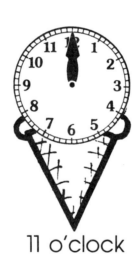

11 o'clock

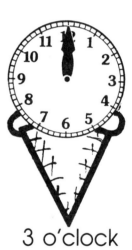

3 o'clock

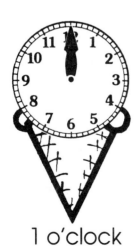

1 o'clock

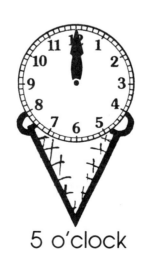

5 o'clock

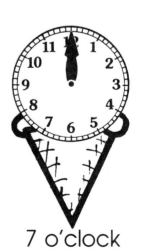

7 o'clock

Name _____

Timely News

Cut out the newspapers at the bottom of the page. Paste each newspaper below the correct clock.

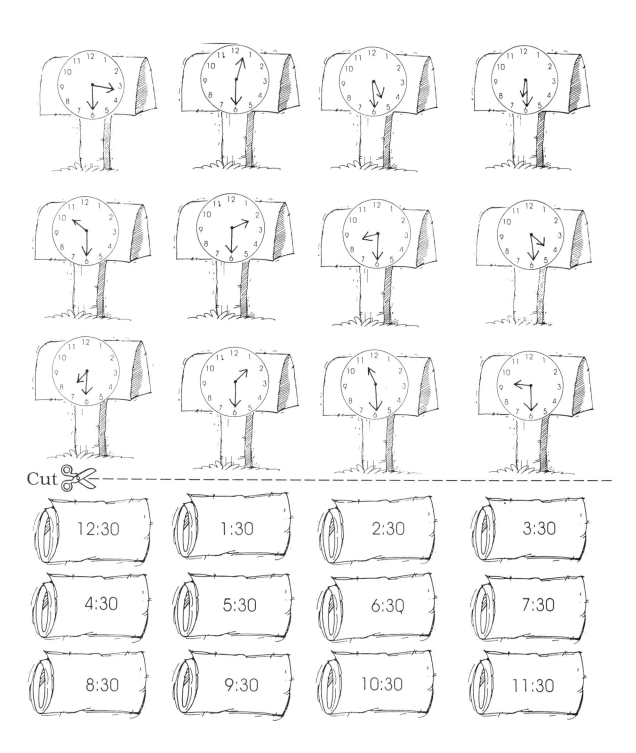

Cut ✂ -

12:30	1:30	2:30	3:30
4:30	5:30	6:30	7:30
8:30	9:30	10:30	11:30

Name _____

Who "Nose" These Times?

Write the time under each clock.
Color the noses.

4:00   4:30

Name _____

Sock Clocks

Draw the hands on the sock clocks.

| 1:30 | 7:00 | 4:30 |

| 10:00 | 3:30 | 9:30 |

| 4:00 | 2:30 | 6:00 |

MATH

Name _____

It's Time to Eat!

Follow the directions
below the clock.

1. Draw a yellow banana at 7:00.
2. Draw a hamburger at 12:00.
3. Draw a red apple at 10:00.
4. Draw a fried egg at 6:00.
5. Draw a hot dog at 11:00.
6. Draw an orange carrot at 1:00.
7. Draw a piece of pizza at 5:00.
8. Draw a donut at 9:00.
9. Draw an ice cream cone with three flavors at 2:00.
10. Draw an ear of corn at 4:00.
11. Draw a chicken leg at 8:00.
12. Draw your favorite food at 3:00.

Name _____

What a Day!

The camp director needs help planning activities for tomorrow afternoon. Read the list carefully. Then use the times to number the activities in the order they will happen.

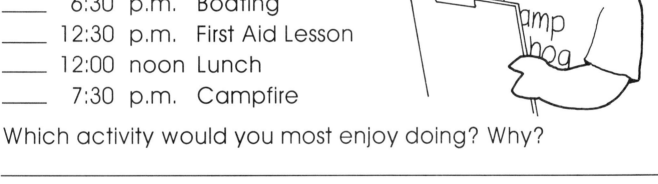

____ 5:30 p.m. Supper
____ 4:30 p.m. Crafts
____ 1:30 p.m. Baseball game
____ 3:00 p.m. Swimming
____ 2:30 p.m. Water Safety
____ 1:00 p.m. Walk in the woods
____ 6:30 p.m. Boating
____ 12:30 p.m. First Aid Lesson
____ 12:00 noon Lunch
____ 7:30 p.m. Campfire

Which activity would you most enjoy doing? Why?

_____

_____

_____

Which activity would you least enjoy doing? Why?

_____

_____

Name _____

It's About Time

There are many ways we measure time. A year is made of 365 days. A week has seven days. A day has 24 hours. An hour is made of 60 minutes. A minute is made of 60 seconds. A second goes very quickly. Can you blink your eyes in one second?

| day | year | minute | week | hour |

Write.

1 ↓ 365 days make a y ___ ___ ___.

2 → Seven days make a w ___ ___ ___.

3 → 24 hours make a d ___ ___.

4 → 60 minutes make an h ___ ___ ___.

5 ↓ 60 seconds make a m ___ ___ ___ ___ ___.

Write the answers in the puzzle above.

Check.

The words in the puzzle tell about ☐ money. ☐ time.

• Write a list of what you can do in **two** minutes.

 IF8693 Super Book for Grade 1

Name _____

Fun Days

There are seven days in a week. Saturday and Sunday are the weekend days. You go to school the other five days. Which day do you like best?

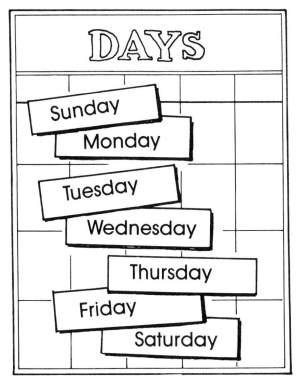

 How many days are in a week?

six   seven   ten

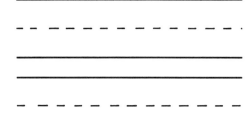 Which two days make a weekend?

| Saturday |
| Thursday |
| Sunday |

_____

– – – – – – – – – –

_____

– – – – – – – – – –

_____

the five days you go to school.

• Draw and color what you do on a weekend.

                   IF8693 Super Book for Grade 1

Name _____

Hmm, What Month Is It?

There are twelve months in a year. The first month is January. The last month is December. Some months have 31 days. Some months have 30 days. February is the shortest month with 28 days. Can you name the months of the year?

☐ April
☐ October
☐ December
☐ July
☐ March
[1] January
☐ May
☐ September
☐ June
☐ February
☐ August
☐ November

Check.

How many months are in a year?

☐ five
☐ nine
☐ twelve

Write.

_____   _____
         first month   last month

Circle.

Yes or No

Some months have 30 days.   Yes   No
Some months have 31 days.   Yes   No
February is the longest month.   Yes   No
February has 28 days.   Yes   No

Write **1-12** in the ☐'s to put the months in order.

• Write the names of the twelve months in the correct order.

Name _____

How Did You Do That?

You use many parts of your body to do even the simplest activities.

Read each activity and write the body parts you would use to do that activity.

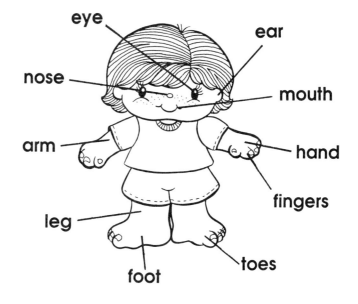

Activities:

1. read a book

_____
_____

2. talk to your friend on the phone

_____
_____

3. put on your hat

_____
_____

4. blow out the candles on a cake

_____
_____

5. eat an ice-cream cone

_____
_____

6. ride a bike to school

_____
_____

     IF8693 Super Book for Grade 1

SCIENCE

Name _____

Body Buddies

Arrange the numbers to print a word that is part of your body. Then color each part.

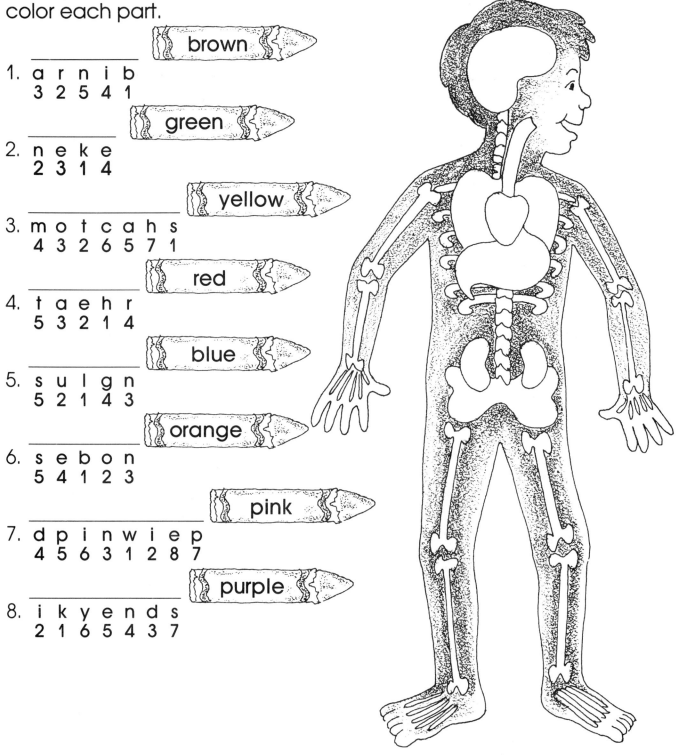

brown

1. _____
   a r n i b
   3 2 5 4 1

green

2. _____
   n e k e
   2 3 1 4

yellow

3. _____
   m o t c a h s
   4 3 2 6 5 7 1

red

4. _____
   t a e h r
   5 3 2 1 4

blue

5. _____
   s u l g n
   5 2 1 4 3

orange

6. _____
   s e b o n
   5 4 1 2 3

pink

7. _____
   d p i n w i e p
   4 5 6 3 1 2 8 7

purple

8. _____
   i k y e n d s
   2 1 6 5 4 3 7

Name _____

It Makes Sense to Me

Our five senses help us understand and make "sense" of our world. Look at each group of pictures. Decide which sense (**see, hear, smell, taste, or feel**) is used for most items in each group of pictures. Write the sense on the line below each group. Then put an **X** on the one picture that does not belong in each group.

SCIENCE

Name _____

Outfitted for Health

Read the phrases in the Word Bank. Write only the **good** health habits on the lines.

Word Bank	Take a bath. Drink water. Sit all day. Exercise.	Eat a lot of sweets Get plenty of sleep. Never wash your hands. Eat healthy foods.	Stay up all night. Keep cuts clean. Brush your teeth.

1. _____

2. _____

3. _____

4. _____

5. _____

6. _____

7. _____

Name _____

Exercise!

Do you like to exercise? Exercise is good for you. Walking and running are good ways to exercise. So are swimming and biking. Some people like to do push-ups, sit-ups and jumping jacks. Exercise can help you feel good. It can make your body stronger, too. What is your favorite kind of exercise?

Unscramble.

_____ is good for you.

s r E c x i e e
7 4 1 5 2 6 3 8

Write.

| walking |
| swimming |
| biking |
| running |

_____

_____

_____

_____

Check.

What do some people do for exercise?

☐ push-ups ☐ sleep ☐ jumping jacks ☐ sit-ups

Circle.

Yes or No

Exercise can help you feel good.	Yes	No
Exercise is very easy.	Yes	No
Exercise can make your body stronger.	Yes	No

• Draw a picture of **you** exercising.

SCIENCE

Name _____

Pyramiding Foods

Read the names of the foods in the Word Bank. Write the words on the lines under the correct food group.

Word Bank: carrots, cherries, chicken, cheese, fish, ham, cake, lettuce, bagel, oranges, pears, rolls, beans, toast, pie, yogurt, candy bar, cottage cheese

dairy

meats

fruits

sweets

vegetables

grains

Name _____

Leaf Shapes

All leaves are not the same. They have different shapes. There are four common shapes.

Draw a line to match the leaf with its shape.

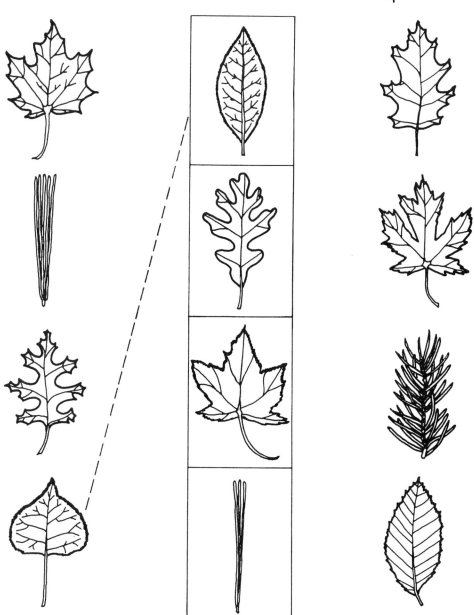

Find some leaves outside.
Try to match them to the shapes.

SCIENCE

Name _____

Tree Parts

Trees have three main parts. They are the trunk, the roots, and the leaves. Each part has a special job. Each part helps the tree.

Cut out the name of each part.

Cut out the job of each part.

Paste them on the picture.

Color the tree.

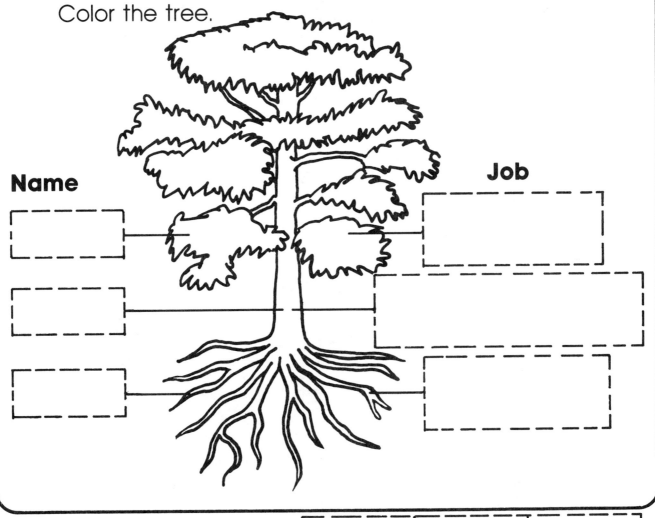

Name

Job

trunk	leaves	roots

| I hold the tree in the ground. | I make food for the tree. | I hold most of the tree above the ground. |

     IF8693 Super Book for Grade 1

Name _____

Leaf Study

Put a leaf under the box on this paper. Rub the paper with the side of your crayon. Use the ruler at the bottom to measure your leaf.

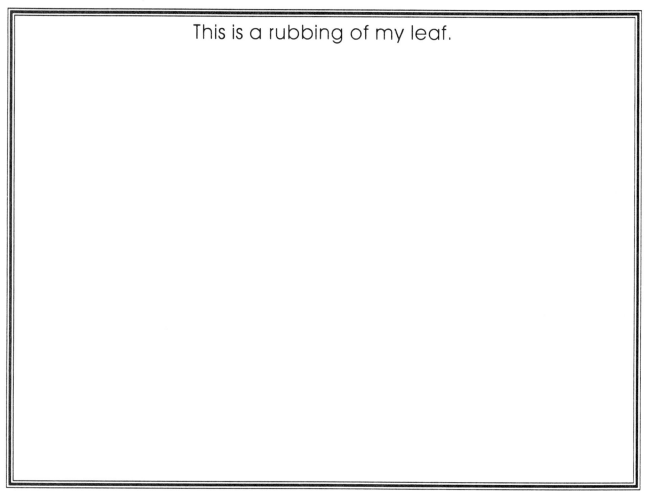

This is a rubbing of my leaf.

1. The color of my leaf is _____ .

2. My leaf is _____ cm wide and _____ cm long.

3. My leaf feels like _____ .

4. I found my leaf _____ .

Name _____

Food Factories

Green leaves are like little factories. They make food for the tree. Leaves need sunshine, air, and water to make food.

Leaves change in the fall. They lose their green color. Then they cannot make food for the tree.

Draw a leaf.
This leaf can make food.
Color it green.

Draw another leaf.
This leaf cannot make food.
Color it with pretty fall colors.

Write the correct word.

green yellow
_____

Food is made by _____ leaves.

shade sunshine
_____

Leaves need _____ to make food.

can cannot
_____

Leaves _____ make food in the fall.

Name _____

My Leaf Collection

Attach a leaf and fill in the blanks.

Teacher: Provide each student with three or more copies of this page so booklets can be made.

Tree _____
Location _____
Date _____

SCIENCE

IF8693 Super Book for Grade 1

Name _____

From Acorn to Mighty Oak

Some trees drop their seeds in the spring. Other trees drop their seeds in the fall. The seeds grow up. Do you know what they grow up to be?

Show how the acorn grows into a mighty oak tree. Write first, second, or third under the pictures to put them in order. Color the pictures.

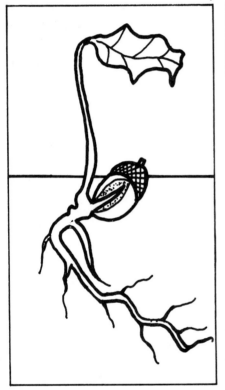 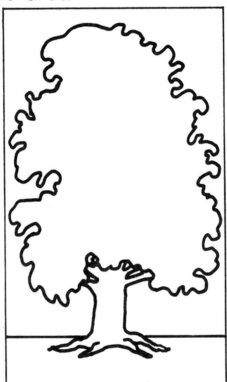 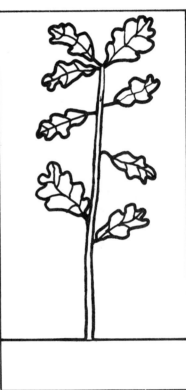

Finish the story.

I am a little acorn. One day

Name _____

Plant Parts

A plant has many parts. Each part has a special job.

Word Bank   roots   stem
                flower   leaf

Label the parts of the plant.

_____

- - - - - - - - - - - - - - - -

_____

_____

- - - - - - - - - - - - - -

_____

_____

- - - - - - - - - - - - - -

_____

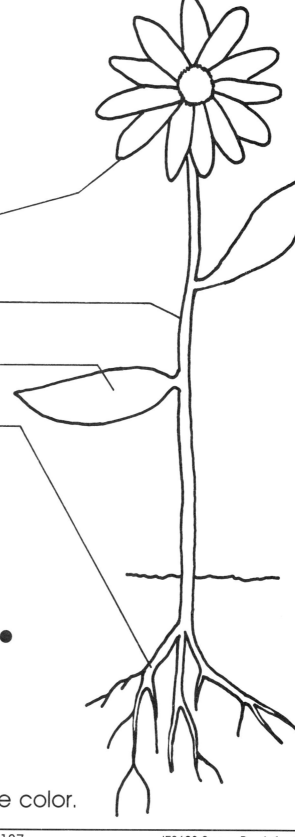

Draw a line from the plant part to its job.

I make the seeds. ●
I make food for the plant. ●
I take water from the roots to the leaves. ●
I hold the plant in the ground. ●

Color the roots red.
Color the stem yellow.
Color the leaves green.
Color the flower your favorite color.

SCIENCE

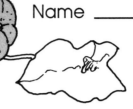

Name _____

Growing Words

Write each word on the line below the correct picture.

pumpkin　　**seed**　　**sprout**　　**flower**　**plant**

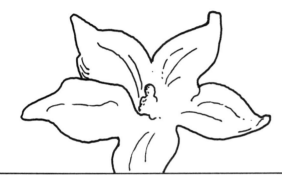

_____

- -

_____

_____

- - - - - - - - - - - - - - - - -

_____

- -

_____

Name _____

Edible Plant Parts

We eat many plant parts. Sometimes we eat just the fruit. Sometimes we eat just the leaves. We also might eat the stem, the root, or the seed.

Draw a line from the picture to the name of the plant part.

Color the plant part.

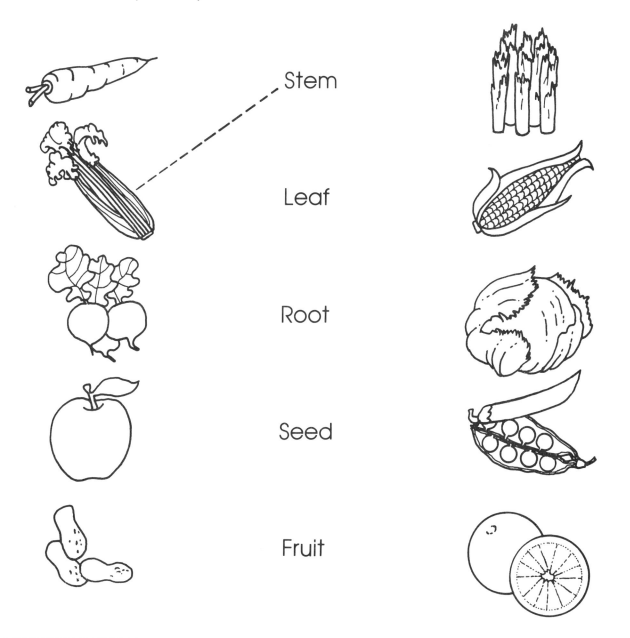

Stem

Leaf

Root

Seed

Fruit

SCIENCE

Name _____

Plant It Right!

Mr. Right and Mr. Wrong planted gardens. Mr. Right planted his garden in the sun. Mr. Wrong planted his garden in the shade. Both of them gave their gardens love and care.

Draw what Mr. Right's garden will look like.

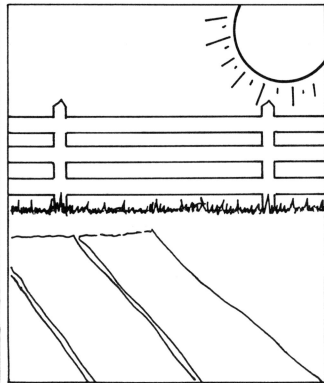

Draw what Mr. Wrong's garden will look like.

Name _____

Water, Please!

Mrs. Right planted her flower seeds last week. She planted them in the sun. She gave her flowers water.

Draw what Mrs. Right's flowers will look like.

Mrs. Wrong planted her flower seeds last week. She planted them in the sun. But she forgot to give them water.

Draw what Mrs. Wrong's flowers will look like.

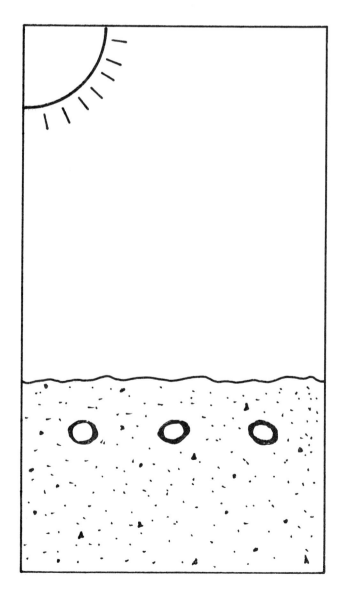
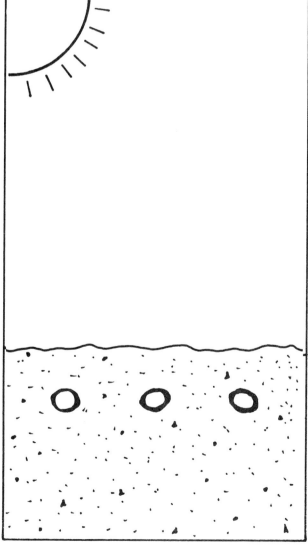

SCIENCE

Name _____

All in the Family

Put an **X** on the animal that does not belong.

1.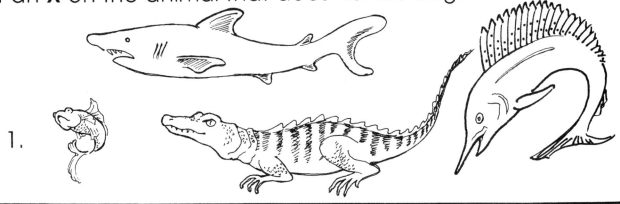

2.

3.

4.

5.

     IF8693 Super Book for Grade 1

Name _____

Animals on the Go

How do these animals move?

Write **walk**, **fly** or **swim**.

_____   _____   _____

_____   _____   _____

_____   _____   _____

SCIENCE

       IF8693 Super Book for Grade 1

Name _____

Pond Community

Many animals make their homes in a pond community, but some of the animals in this picture do not belong.

Draw an **X** on the animals that do **not** belong.

Name _____

Grassland Community

Many animals make their homes in a grassland community, but some of the animals in this picture do not belong.

Draw an **X** on the animals that do **not** belong.

IF8693 Super Book for Grade 1

SCIENCE

Name _____

Ocean Community

Many animals make their homes in an ocean community, but some of the animals in this picture do not belong.

Draw an **X** on the animals that do **not** belong.

Name _____

Forest Community

Many animals make their homes in a forest community, but some of the animals in this picture do not belong.

Draw an **X** on the animals that do **not** belong.

SCIENCE

Name _____

Animals at Home

Did you ever see a fish living in a tree? Of course you didn't! Fish live in the water. Help the animals find their homes.

Cut out each animal.
Paste it on its home.
Color the picture.

squirrel   robin   fish   bee

Name _____

Where's My Baby?

Match the adult animal to the baby animal!

sheep

cat

hen

pig

dog

duck

cow

goose

goat

horse

chick

calf

gosling

kitten

piglet

duckling

kid

lamb

puppy

foal

SCIENCE

Name _____

Feathered Friends

Name the parts of the bird.

_____

_____

_____

_____

Read the riddle. Name each bird part.

I keep a bird warm and dry. What am I? _____

I help a bird stand or swim. What am I? _____

I help a bird eat. What am I? _____

I make a bird fly high in the sky. What am I? _____

Word Bank			
feathers	feet	bill	wings

Name _____

My Bird List

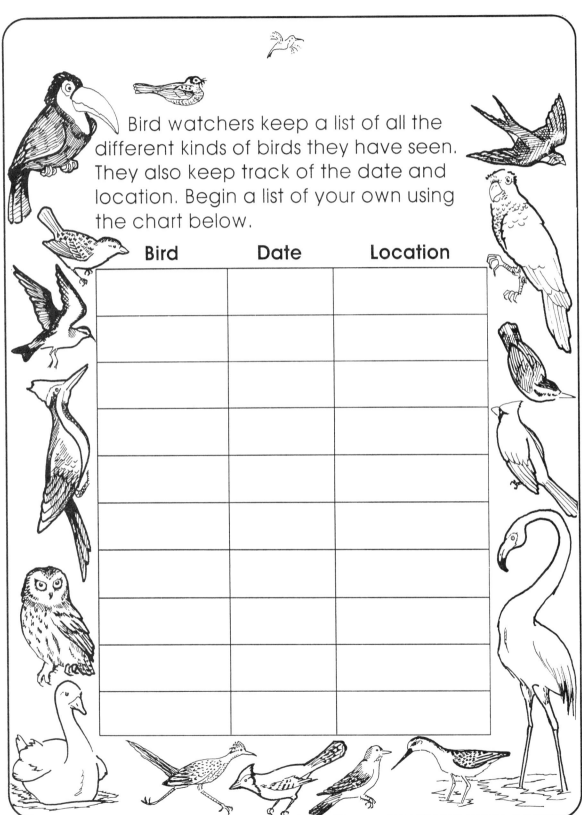

Bird watchers keep a list of all the different kinds of birds they have seen. They also keep track of the date and location. Begin a list of your own using the chart below.

Bird	Date	Location

SCIENCE

Name _____

I Slither and Crawl

Do the puzzle about reptiles.
Color only the reptiles.

Across

2. A reptile's skin has _____ .

5. A _____ is a reptile with no legs.

Down

1. A _____ is a reptile with a hard shell on its back.

3. Reptiles are _____ -blooded animals.

4. Baby reptiles hatch from _____ .

Word Bank				
eggs	cold	scales	snake	turtle

IF8693 Super Book for Grade 1

Name _____

A Reptile Riddle

Circle the animal that does not belong in the group. Print the letters beside the circled words in the spaces below to find the answer to the riddle.

Birds
1. L robin
   N bluebird
   I cow
   J crow

Insects
2. L snake
   A ladybug
   N wasp
   T bee

Dogs
3. B collie
   I beagle
   S shepherd
   L ox

Reptiles
4. R snake
   I horse
   G turtle
   W alligator

Farm Animals
5. G tiger
   K pig
   O cow
   Y hen

Jungle Animals
6. J lion
   B cheetah
   U tiger
   A rat

Zoo Animals
7. M bear
   O giraffe
   T dog
   F zebra

Ocean Animals
8. H octopus
   T whale
   K shark
   O camel

Fish
9. R raccoon
   I perch
   V catfish
   L tuna

Riddle
What do you call a sick crocodile?

An . . .

___ ___ ___ ___ ___ ___ ___ ___ ___
 1   2   3   4   5   6   7   8   9

Name _____

I'm Slippery and Cold

Do the puzzle about amphibians.

Color only the amphibians.

Down

1. Amphibian babies usually hatch from _____.

2. Amphibians are _____ -blooded animals.

4. Amphibians often have smooth, moist _____.

Across

3. Amphibian babies breathe with either lungs or

_____ .

5. Amphibians live in the water and on _____ .

Word Bank				
land	gills	skin	eggs	cold

Name _____

From Mice to Whales

Do the puzzle about mammals.

Color only the mammals.

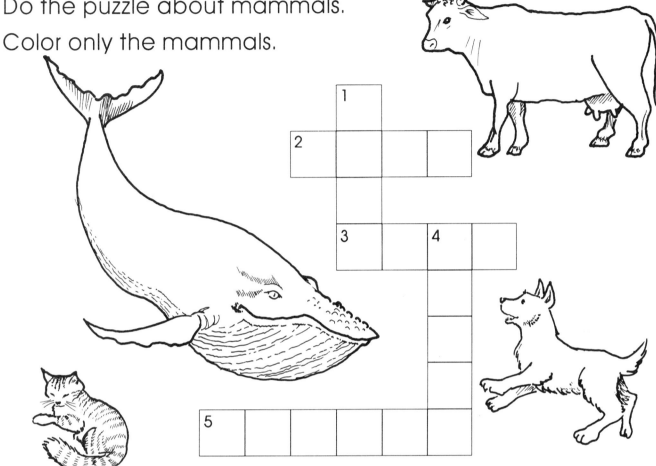

Down

1. Mammals are _____ -blooded.
4. Mammals breathe with _____ .

Across

2. A mammal's body is usually covered with _____ .
3. Mother mammals feed _____ to their babies.
5. Mammal's _____ are born alive.

Word Bank				
hair	babies	lungs	milk	warm

SCIENCE

Name _____

Just Hanging Around

Bats like to fly at night. They sleep in the daytime. A bat sleeps by hanging upside down. Most bats live in trees and caves. Have you ever seen a bat?

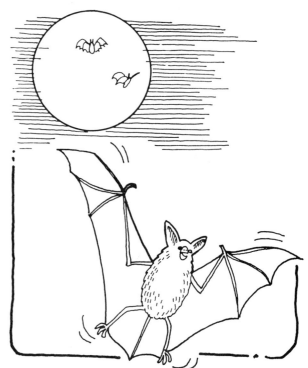

night   noon
_____

- - - - - - - - - - - -

Bats like to fly at _____.

Bats sleep in the   room.
                    daytime.

How do bats sleep?

Most bats live in: ☐ trees
                    ☐ caves
                    ☐ floor

the bats black.

• Draw and color a cave with sleeping bats in it.

Name _____

Crawling with Insects

Do the puzzle about insects.
Color only the insects.

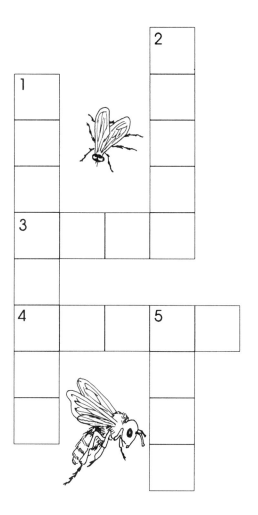

Down
1. Insects have a hard outer _____ .
2. Many insects have two pairs of _____ :
5. Insects have simple and compound _____ :

Across
3. Insects have three pairs of _____ .
4. Insects have _____ main body sections.

```
+-----------------------------------------------+
|                 Word Bank                     |
|   skeleton    legs    wings    three    eyes  |
+-----------------------------------------------+
```

SCIENCE

Name _____

Spinning Spiders

There are many kinds of spiders. Spiders have eight legs. They like to eat insects. Many spiders spin a web. The web is the spider's home. Have you ever seen a spider's web?

eight   four
_____

- - - - - - - - - - - - - -

Spiders have _____ legs.

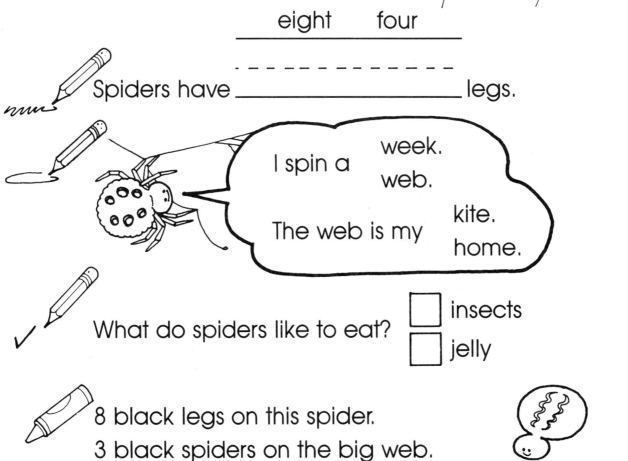

I spin a   week.
             web.

The web is my   kite.
                  home.

What do spiders like to eat?   ☐ insects
                                ☐ jelly

8 black legs on this spider.
3 black spiders on the big web.

• Draw and color a spider and its web.

208   IF8693 Super Book for Grade 1

Name _____

Fish for Me

Do the puzzle about fish.

Color only the fish.

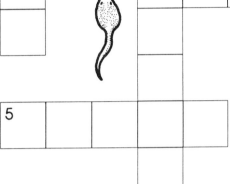

Down

1. Fish have _____ , not legs.
3. A fish's body is often covered with _____ .

Across

2. Fish breathe through _____ .
4. A fish is a _____ -blooded animal.
5. Fish live in the sea and fresh _____ .

Word Bank				
water	scales	cold	fins	gills

SCIENCE

Name _____

"Hatch" Something Up

Many animals are hatched from eggs.

Read the clues. Then use the Word Bank to write the name of the correct animal on each egg.

I am a reptile.
I have big, sharp teeth.
I live near a river.

I live most of my life in water.
I eat tadpoles and water insects.
I can pull myself inside my shell.

I have feathers.
I have webbed feet.
I swim in a pond.
I quack with my bill.

I have feathers.
I live on a farm.
I have wings and make peeping
    sounds with my beak.

I live near water.
I eat insects.
I have a tail when I hatch,
    but I lose it as I grow.
I can leap up to six feet.

Word Bank

snake

chick

frog

mud turtle

duck

alligator

Name _____

Butterfly – Part 1

Cut out the butterfly.
Cut out the egg.
Paste them on the milkweed leaf.

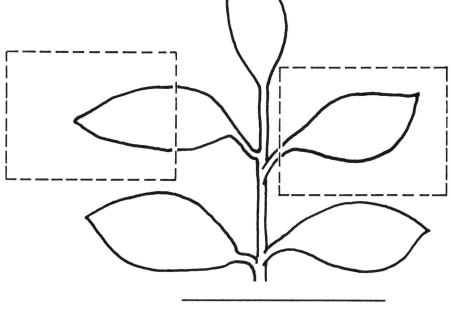

_____

– – – – – – – – – – – – – –

The butterfly lays one _____ on a milkweed

_____

– – – – – – – – – –

_____ .

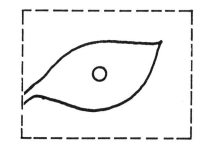

Word Bank

leaf

egg

Name _____

Butterfly – Part 2

Cut out the caterpillar.
Paste it on the milkweed leaf.
Color the caterpillar black, white, and yellow.

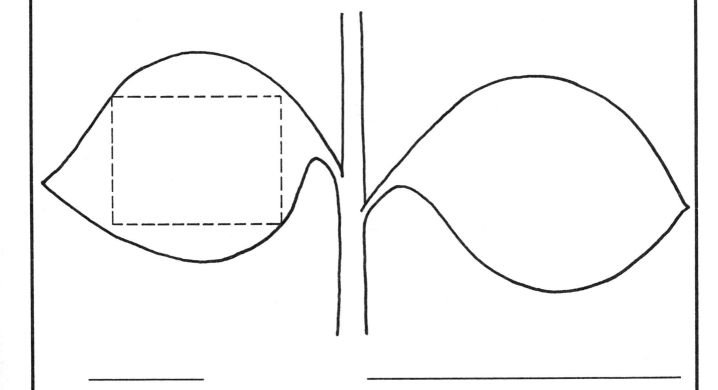

_____   _____

The _____ hatches into a _____.

 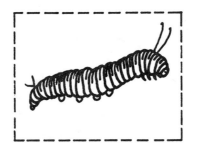

Word Bank
egg
caterpillar

Name _____

Butterfly – Part 3

Cut out the caterpillar and its food.
Paste them on the milkweed plant.

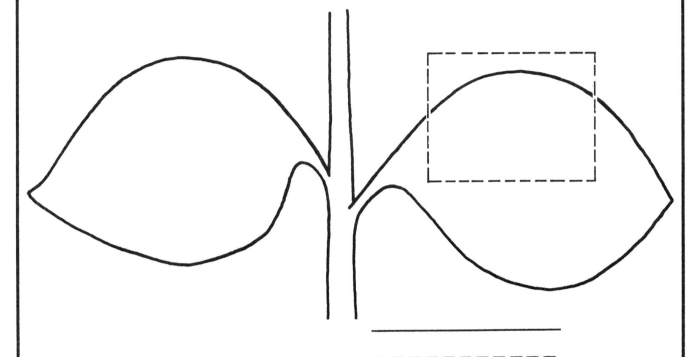

The hungry caterpillar eats the _____ .

The caterpillar is _____ .

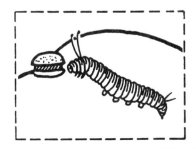

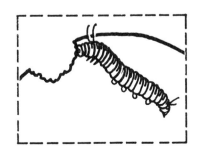

Word Bank

leaf
growing

Name _____

Butterfly – Part 4

Cut out the chrysalis.
Paste it in place.

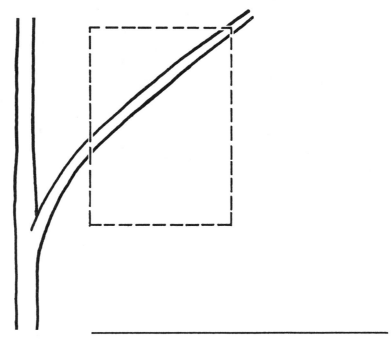

_____
- - - - - - - - - - - - - - -
The caterpillar is ready to _____ .

_____
- - - - - - - - - - - - - - -
It forms a pale _____ chrysalis.

- -

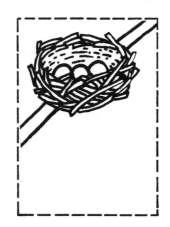

Word Bank

green
change

Name _____

Butterfly – Part 5

Cut out the butterfly.
Paste it in place.

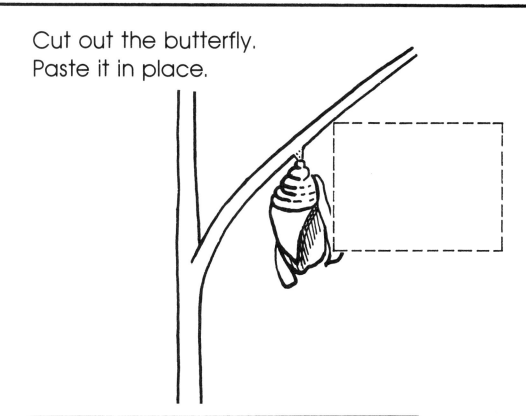

The _____ is now a butterfly.

The _____ flies away.

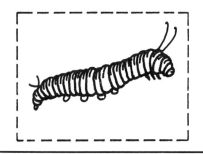

Word Bank

butterfly
caterpillar

Name _____

Metamorphosis

Show how the monarch changes.
Cut out the pictures.
Paste them in order.

Word Bank
butterfly

_____

- - - - - - - - - - - - - - - - -

The life cycle of a _____
is called metamorphosis.

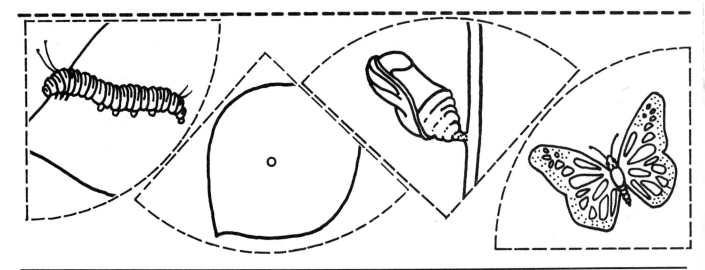

Name _____

Migration

Cut out the animals.
Paste them in place.

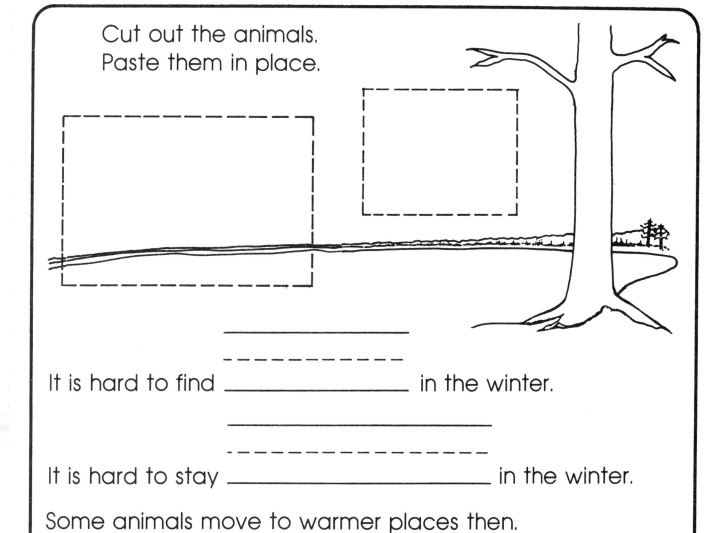

_____

It is hard to find _____ in the winter.

_____

It is hard to stay _____ in the winter.

Some animals move to warmer places then.
This is called migration.

SCIENCE

Word Bank

warm
food

Name _____

Active Animals

Cut out the animals.
Paste them in place.

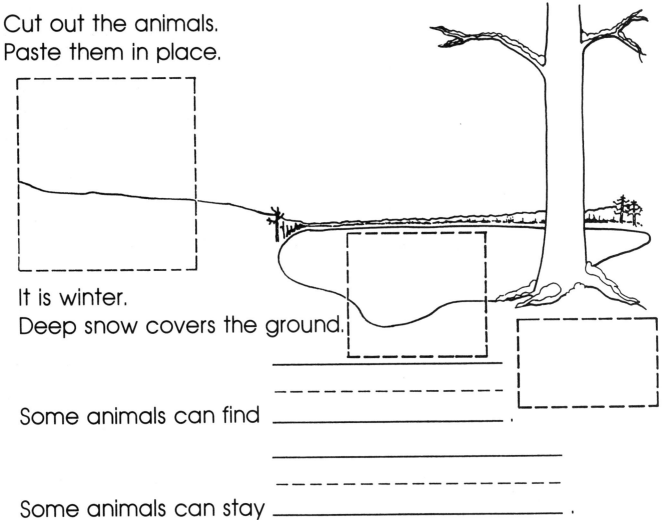

It is winter.
Deep snow covers the ground.

Some animals can find _____ .

Some animals can stay _____ .

These animals stay active in winter.

Word Bank
food
warm

Name _____

Storing Food

Cut out the beaver.
Paste him by the hole in the ice.
Trace the path to the beaver's lodge.

_____
- - - - - - - - - - - - - - - - -

Some animals store food for _____ .

_____
- - - - - - - - - - - - - - - - -

The beaver stores food in his _____ .

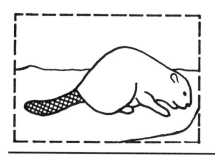

Word Bank

lodge
winter

IF8693 Super Book for Grade 1

Name _____

Hibernation

Cut out the fat woodchuck.
Paste him by his hole.
Trace the path to the
woodchuck's home.

Some animals hibernate in the winter.

_____
_ _ _ _ _ _ _ _ _ _ _

The woodchuck grows a layer of _____ in the fall.

_____
_ _ _ _ _ _ _ _ _ _ _

His heartbeat goes _____. His temperature goes

_____   _____
_ _ _ _ _ _ _ _   _ _ _ _ _ _ _ _

_____. He stays in his home while it is _____.

Word Bank
cold
fat
down
down

Name _____

Animals in Winter

Cut out the animal.
Paste it in its place.
Write the animal's name.

This animal hibernates in the winter.

_____

- - - - - - - - - - - - - - - -

_____

This animal migrates in the winter.

_____

- - - - - - - - - - - - - - - -

_____

This animal stays active in the winter.

_____

- - - - - - - - - - - - - - - -

_____

This animal stores food for the winter.

_____

- - - - - - - - - - - - - - - -

_____

SCIENCE

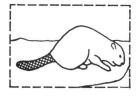   

Word Bank

rabbit
bird
beaver
woodchuck

Name _____

Animal Homes

Follow the directions below to finish the picture.

1. Draw a fish in the lake.

2. Draw a whale in the ocean.

3. Draw a dog beside the river.

4. Draw a goat on the mountain.

5. Draw a bird on the island.

6. Now color the picture.

Name _____

Blooms and Birds

It is warm in the spring. Flowers begin to bloom. Trees have new  . Birds make their nests and lay eggs. Do you like to fly a kite in the spring?

warm   last

It is _____ in the spring.

What can you see in the spring?

What do birds do in the spring?

☐ Birds make nests.

☐ They lay eggs.

☐ They wash dishes.

• Draw and color a nest with four eggs in it.

223   IF8693 Super Book for Grade 1

SCIENCE

Name _____

Fun in the Sun

Summer can be very
hot. It is the time when kids
are out of school. They have
fun playing with friends,
swimming to keep cool,
and sometimes going on
family picnics and vacations.

purple   hot

_____

Summer can be very _____.

What happens in the summer?

☐ Kids are out of school.

☐ Skunks go on picnics.

☐ Kids play with friends.

What do you like to do in the summer?

_____

_____

_____

• Draw and color a picture of your family on vacation.

Name _____

Autumn Leaves

The air gets cool in the autumn. Kids go back to school. Animals store food for the winter. Leaves turn red, yellow and orange. It is a pretty time of the year.

time   cool
_____
- - - - - - - - - - -

The air gets _____ in the autumn.

What happens in the autumn?

☐ Kids go back to school.

☐ Animals store food.

☐ The air is very hot.

red   yellow   orange

• Draw and color an autumn tree.

225   IF8693 Super Book for Grade 1

Name _____

Winter Warm-ups

Winter can be cold and snowy. Animals stay near each other to keep warm. People wear coats, hats and . Kids can make a snowman. It is fun to play in the snow.

Winter can be: ☐ cold
                ☐ snowy
                ☐ purple

like   warm

We try to stay _____.

What do people wear in the winter?

gloves   hat   pan   coat

a black 🎩 on the ⛄.

• Draw and color a snowman.

Name _____

The Four Seasons

1. Cut out and paste the season words on the correct boxes below.

2. Color the clothes for:
   Fall – blue; Winter – red;
   Spring – green; Summer – yellow

Fall

Winter

SCIENCE

Name _____

Frederick's Furry Friends

Draw picture details of the four seasons around each of Frederick's furry friends. the pictures and each mouse.

Spring Mouse

Summer Mouse

Fall Mouse

Winter Mouse

Name _____

Magnetic Attraction

Draw a line from the magnet to each thing that it can pull.

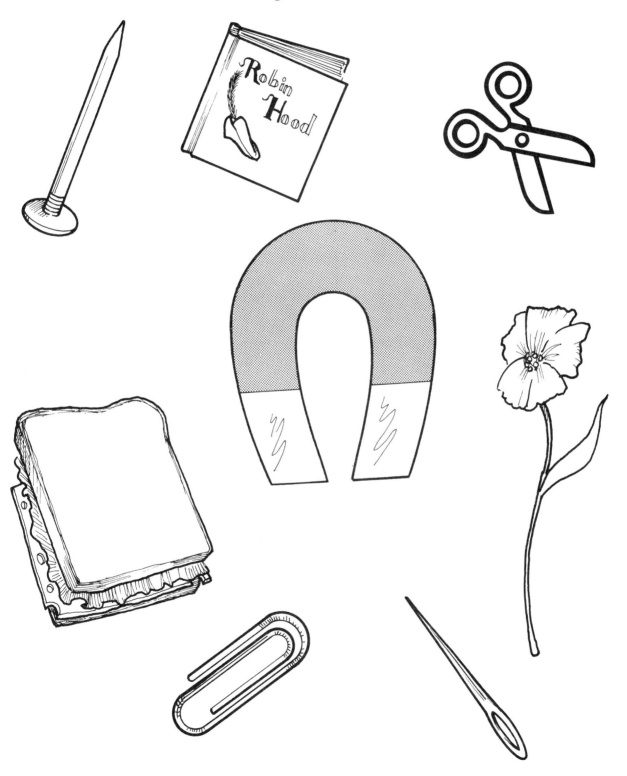

Name _____

Sticky Hunt

What things will a magnet stick to?

Make lists of the things in your room that will and will not stick to a magnet.

Magnets stick to:	Magnets do not stick to:
_____	_____
_____	_____
_____	_____
_____	_____
_____	_____
_____	_____
_____	_____

Caution: Do not try your magnet on these things.

TV	Computer disks
VCR	Cassette tapes
Computer	Video tapes
Radio	Credit cards
Tape recorder	Telephone

Opposites Attract

Every magnet has a north pole and a south pole. When you hold two magnets together, this is what happens:

If a north pole and a south pole are next to each other, the magnets attract each other.

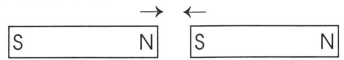

If two north poles or two south poles are next to each other, the magnets repel each other.

Tell what each pair of magnets below will do. If the magnets will attract each other, color them red. If the magnets will repel each other, color them blue.

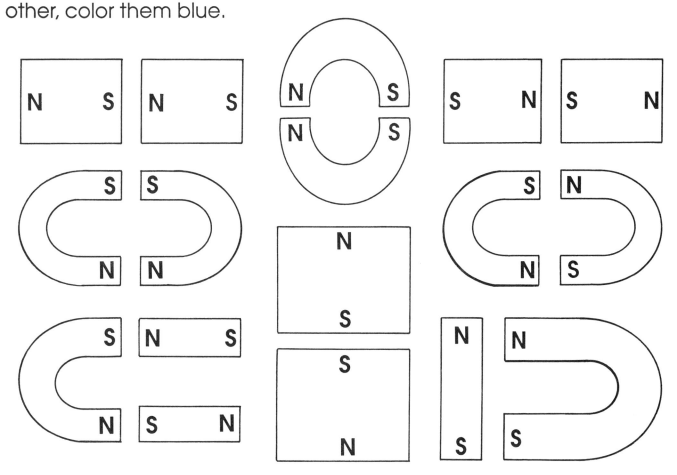

 IF8693 Super Book for Grade 1

SCIENCE

Name _____

Our Planet Earth

Earth is a planet. It is the planet where we live. Earth has land and water. It gets light and heat from the sun. Earth has one moon. Many people think there is life on other planets. Earth is the only planet that we know has life. Do **you** think there is life on other planets?

Unscramble.

Earth is the _____ where we live.

l e t p n a
2 5 6 1 4 3

Check.

☐ I have land and water.
☐ I get light and heat from the sun.
☐ I have five moons.
☐ I have one moon.
☐ I am a planet.

Circle.

Earth is the only planet that we know has   stars.
life.

Color.

Draw one yellow moon in the picture.

• Draw and color a picture of Earth.

Name _____

Man on the Moon

Do you ever look at the moon at night? The moon travels around the Earth. It gets its light from the sun. Men have gone to the moon in spaceships. They have walked on the moon. They even came back with moon rocks to study. Would you like to walk on the moon?

Circle.
The moon travels around the room.
Earth.

Write.
The moon gets its light from the _____.
Earth   sun

Check.
How did men go to the moon? ☐ spaceships
☐ automobiles

Circle.
Yes or No
Men have walked on the moon.   **Yes   No**

Circle.
What did men bring back from the moon?   stars
rocks

Color.
Draw a red spaceship on the moon.

• Draw what you would do if you went to the moon.

SCIENCE

Name _____

A Falling Star

Have you ever seen a falling star? Falling stars are not really stars. They are small pieces of rock. As falling stars fall, they get hot and burn. They look big because they give off so much light. That is why they are so bright in the night sky. Did you know that meteor is another name for a falling star?

Circle.
Yes or No

A falling star is really a star.	Yes	No
Falling stars are pieces of rock.	Yes	No
Falling stars burn as they fall.	Yes	No

Check.
Why does a falling star give off light?

☐ It gets hot and burns.

☐ It has a light bulb in it.

Unscramble.
Another name for a falling star is _____.

e r m o t e
2 6 1 5 3 4

Color.
Draw two yellow falling stars in the picture.

• Write a poem about a falling star.

Name _____

Far Out!

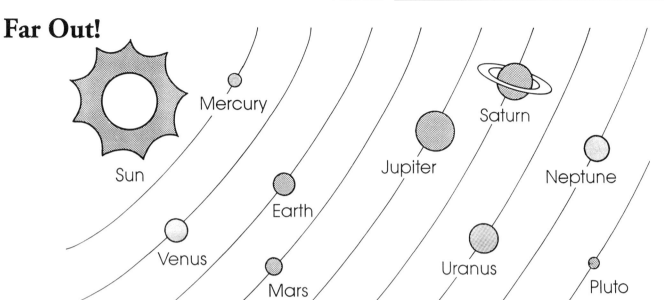

Imagine that you are traveling from the sun to outer space. Write Sun first. Then write the names of the planets in order starting with Mercury.

1. _ _ _ _ _ _ _ _ _ _ _ _

2. _ _ _ _ _ _ _ _ _ _ _ _

3. _ _ _ _ _ _ _ _ _ _ _ _

4. _ _ _ _ _ _ _ _ _ _ _ _

5. _ _ _ _ _ _ _ _ _ _ _ _

6. _ _ _ _ _ _ _ _ _ _ _ _

7. _ _ _ _ _ _ _ _ _ _ _ _

8. _ _ _ _ _ _ _ _ _ _ _ _

9. _ _ _ _ _ _ _ _ _ _ _ _

10. _ _ _ _ _ _ _ _ _ _ _ _

SCIENCE

Flip Fun!   Draw what you think life could be like on another planet.

Name _____

Twinkling Starlights

Stars change as they get older. They start out big and then shrink. As they shrink, they change color. Color the stars the correct color.

red

orange

yellow

blue

Look at all of these stars. Color each star the correct color. Then draw a circle around the youngest stars and a box around the oldest ones.

Name _____

Me, Myself, and I

1. Tell about yourself on the lines below.

2. Then draw a picture of yourself.

My name is _____ .

The color of my eyes is _____ .

The color of my hair is _____ .

This is me!

237   IF8693 Super Book for Grade 1

SOCIAL STUDIES

Name _____

I Am Special

1. Color the letters in the word [SPECIAL].

2. Cut and paste [SPECIAL] in the [___] below.

3. Color the objects below.

4. Write a story telling why you are special.

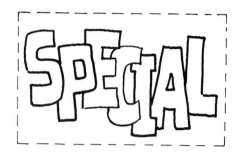

I am [___] because:

_____
- -
_____
_____
_____
- -
_____
- -

Name _____

All About Me

Color and write.

My name
_____
- -

My school
_____
- -

My street
_____
- -

My phone
_____
- -

My city
_____
- -

My state
_____
- -

SOCIAL STUDIES

Name _____

Birthday Surprise!

1. Complete sentences 1 and 2.

2. Connect the numbers in the dot-to-dot.

3. Color 2 presents red and 3 presents blue.

4. Draw candles on the dot-to-dot picture to show how old you are.

5. Color the dot-to-dot.

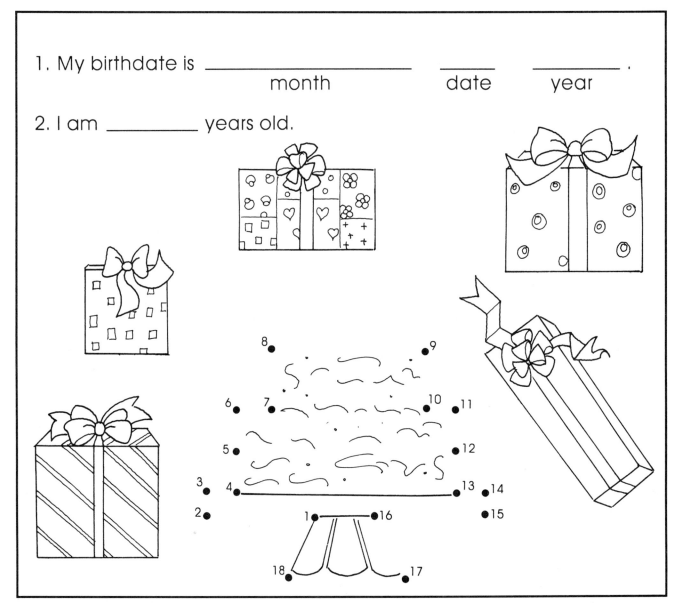

1. My birthdate is _____   _____   _____ .
   month   date   year

2. I am _____ years old.

Name _____

Birthday Bonus Poster

My Cake

_____'s Birthday

_____ (date)

How I'll Look

Where I'll Celebrate

Friends I'll Invite
(Write their names and draw their pictures.)

My Gifts

TO:
FROM:

Age I'll Be
(Make a big number and decorate it.)

My Birthday Dinner
(Draw what you'd like.)

SOCIAL ST

Name _____

Create a Cinquain — A Poem About Me

Line 1 = 1 word
Line 2 = 2 words describing line 1 (adjectives)
Line 3 = 3 action words (ending in ing)
Line 4 = a phrase expressing a feeling or
       observation about line 1
Line 5 = a word renaming or describing line 1

School
fun, exciting
learning, studying, playing
a great place to be
Elementary

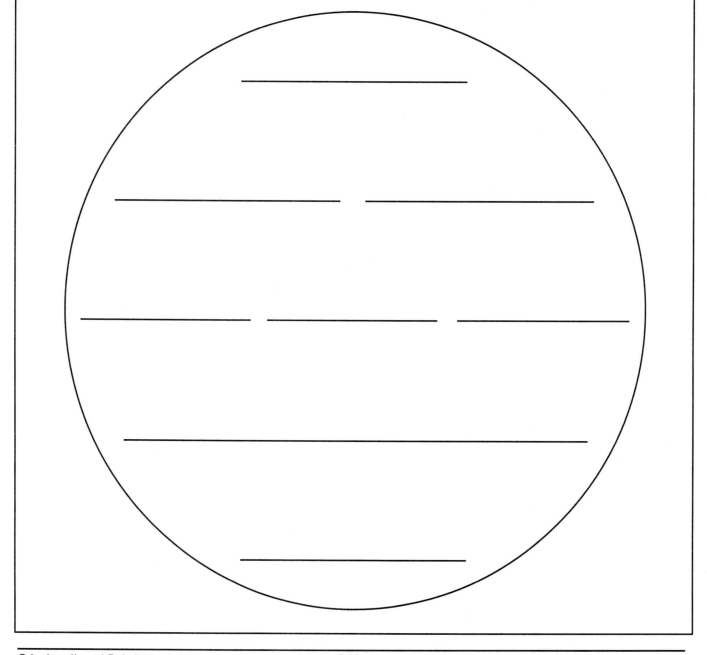

Name _____

Feeling Fantastic!

People can have many
feelings. They can be happy.
They can be sad. Sometimes
people can feel angry.
Everyone has feelings.

 People can have many   five.
                                          feelings.

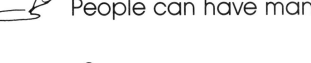

happy
angry
sad

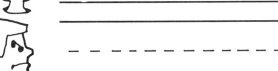

 Make the faces look:

happy 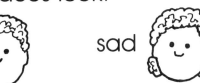   sad   angry

• Draw and color a picture of how you feel.

243   IF8693 Super Book for Grade 1

SOCIAL STUDIES

Name _____

Silly Me

Copy and finish each sentence.

When I feel happy, I...

_____

- -

_____

When I feel sad, I...

_____

- -

_____

When I feel silly, I...

_____

- -

_____

When I feel angry, I...

_____

- -

_____

When I feel scared, I...

_____

- -

_____

When I feel excited, I...

_____

- -

_____

Name _____

My Family

1. Color the roof brown.

2. Color the chimney red.

3. Color the bushes green.

4. Draw a picture of your family inside the house.

5. Write your address at the bottom of the page.

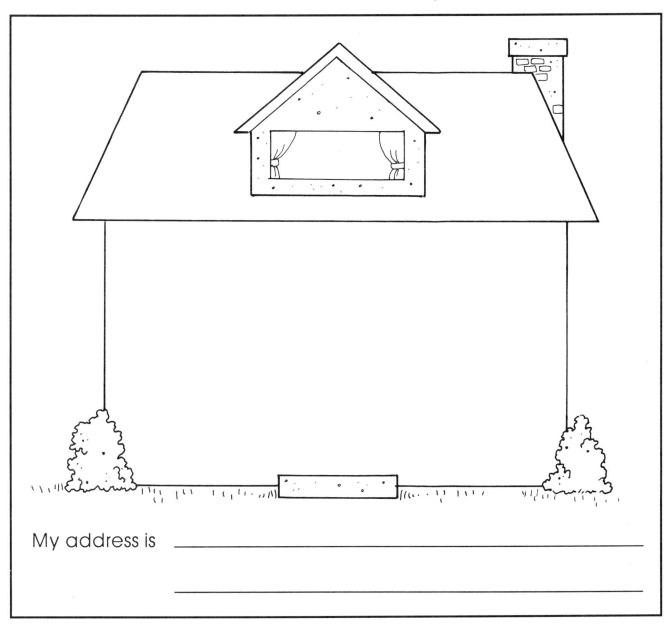

My address is _____

_____

SOCIAL STUDIES

Name _____

Family Puzzle

Draw family members, pets or fun things you do with your family over the entire puzzle. Color. Cut apart and give the whole puzzle to a classmate to put together.

 **"My Mom"** Name _____

Draw a picture of someone in your family.

Write one sentence to tell why this person is special.

_____

_____

_____

Draw a picture of a gift you would like to give this person.

SOCIAL STUDIES

Name _____

Fun with Friends

A friend is someone you like very much. Friends play together. Friends help each other, too. It is nice to have many friends.

_____ friend _____ from

A _____ is someone you like.

Yes or No

Friends play together.	Yes	No
Friends are cars.	Yes	No
Friends help each other.	Yes	No

Which are friends?

• Draw and color a picture of you and your friends.

248

Name _____

Dressed and Ready

1. Draw a picture of you and a friend going to school.

2. Dress you and your friend correctly for the weather.

3. Write your school's name on the sign.

SOCIAL STUDIES

Name _____

Special People

Use the code to name the special people below.

A	C	D	E	F	G	H	I	L	M	O	P	R	T
1	2	3	4	5	6	7	8	9	10	11	12	13	14

Name _____

What's My Job?

 the correct word on each line.  a line to match the sentence.

pilot   farmer   doctor   builder   plumber   teacher

_____

A _____ helps us learn new things.

_____

A _____ flies planes many places.

_____

A _____ plants and grows crops.

_____

A _____ fixes many leaky pipes.

_____

A _____ builds new buildings.

_____

A _____ helps people get well.

the pictures.

SOCIAL STUDIES

Name _____

My Teacher Helps Me Learn . . .

1. Circle the words from the Word Bank in the puzzle.
2. Then color the circled words green.
3. Last, write your teacher's name on the bottom line.

Word Bank

spelling	science	writing	reading	music
art	math	gym	social studies	

r	e	a	d	i	n	g	w	r	i	t	i	n	g
s	o	c	i	a	l	s	t	u	d	i	e	s	x
w	t	y	s	p	e	l	l	i	n	g	b	z	p
o	p	v	s	c	i	e	n	c	e	j	l	x	q
v	w	p	w	m	u	s	i	c	p	q	h	i	r
b	s	c	t	m	a	t	h	w	q	x	z	l	y
t	u	o	a	p	a	r	t	h	o	n	f	k	m
k	m	r	s	z	g	y	m	e	c	d	o	b	n

_____

- - - - - - - - - - - - - - - -

My teacher's name is _____ .

                   IF8693 Super Book for Grade 1

Name _____

Firefighter Find

A firefighter uses many things in his or her job.

Find the words from the Word Bank in the burning house below.

Word Bank			
boots	hat	oxygen mask	gloves
ax	hose	fire engine	ladder

SOCIAL STUDIES

Name _____

In the Cockpit

A pilot is a person who can fly an airplane. A pilot went to a special school to learn to fly a plane. Some pilots fly planes for fun. Some pilots fly planes as their jobs. A pilot sits in a special part of the plane called the cockpit. Have you ever seen a pilot sitting in the cockpit of a plane?

Write.

The person who flies an airplane is a _____.

point   pilot

Circle.

Yes or No

A pilot went to a special school.	Yes	No
Some pilots fly just for fun.	Yes	No
A pilot drives a school bus.	Yes	No
Some pilots fly planes as their jobs.	Yes	No

Circle.

Where does a pilot sit to fly an airplane?

 cockpit

 bench

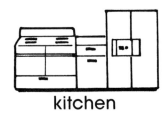 kitchen

Color.

Put green **X**'s on the pilots.

• Draw a picture of a cockpit with **you** as the pilot.

Name _____

On the Farm

Farmers have a very important job. They grow most of the food that we eat. Some farmers grow plants such as oats, corn and wheat. Some farmers raise animals for food. They sell milk from cows. They sell eggs from chickens. Many farmers use machines to help them do their work.

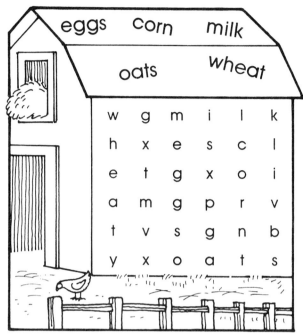

eggs   corn   milk
oats   wheat

w	g	m	i	l	k
h	x	e	s	c	l
e	t	g	x	o	i
a	m	g	p	r	v
t	v	s	g	n	b
y	x	o	a	t	s

Circle.

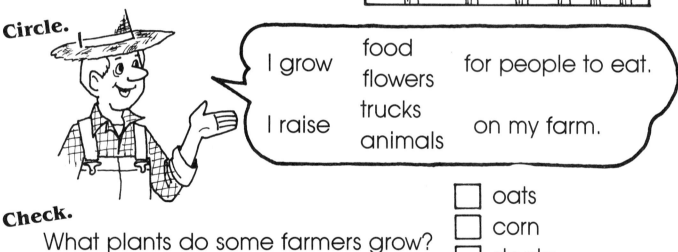

I grow   food / flowers   for people to eat.

I raise   trucks / animals   on my farm.

Check.

What plants do some farmers grow?

☐ oats
☐ corn
☐ steaks
☐ wheat

Match.

Which food comes from which animal?

milk   chickens

eggs   cows

Circle the words in the puzzle above.

• Draw a picture of three farm animals.

               IF8693 Super Book for Grade 1

SOCIAL STUDIES

Name _____

We Care for You

Doctors help many people. They help sick people get well. They help healthy people stay well. People go to special schools to learn to be doctors. There are many kinds of doctors. There are doctors for children, eye doctors, ear doctors, bone doctors and heart doctors. Would you like to be a doctor?

1→bone

2↓eye

1→

3→

4→

3→heart

4→ear

Check.

How does a doctor help people?

☐ A doctor helps sick people get well.

☐ A doctor helps people build houses.

☐ A doctor helps healthy people stay well.

Unscramble.

There are many kinds of _____. Some doctors are

```
c t o d o s r
3 4 2 1 5 7 6
```

just for _____.

```
h d n c l e r i
2 5 8 1 4 7 6 3
```

Match.

eye doctor
ear doctor
bone doctor
heart doctor

Write.

Fill in the puzzle.

• Write a list of three things you do to stay healthy.

Name _____

Explorers of Space

An astronaut is a person who travels in space. Only a few people can become astronauts. They must be in very good health. They must be very smart. There are special schools to train astronauts. Some astronauts are scientists. Some are pilots. They must work hard to be ready to travel in space.

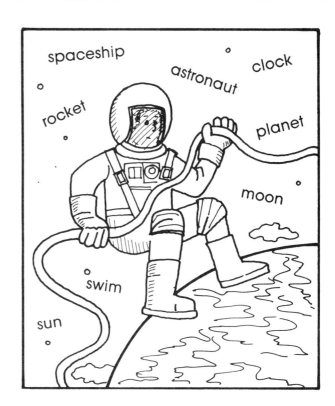

Unscramble.

A person who travels in space is an _____.

r t n o t s a u a
4 9 6 5 3 2 1 8 7

Check.

☐ Everyone can become an astronaut.
☐ An astronaut must be in very good health.
☐ An astronaut must be very smart.
☐ There are special schools to train astronauts.

Circle.

Some astronauts are: scientists
                        judges
                        pilots

Color.

Put a red circle around the **space** words in the picture.

• Draw a picture of where you would like to go in space.

257   IF8693 Super Book for Grade 1

SOCIAL STUDIES

Name _____

When I Grow Up . . .

Draw a line to the correct answer.

1. I want to help sick people. policeman

2. I want to fly a plane. teacher

3. I want to help people learn. artist

4. I want to be in movies. pilot

5. I want to keep people safe. doctor

6. I want to help sick animals. actor

7. I want to paint pretty pictures. vet

Name _____

I Want to Be . . .

1. Draw a picture of what you might look like when you grow up.

2. Then write what you want to be when you are grown up and why.

When I grow up I want to be a

_____

because . . . _____

_____

_____

_____

_____

_____

_____

_____

SOCIAL STUDIES

Name _____

Making a Map

1. Color and cut out the symbols.

2. Paste the symbols next to the matching words in the map key.

3. Then color the rest of the map.

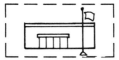   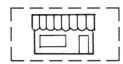

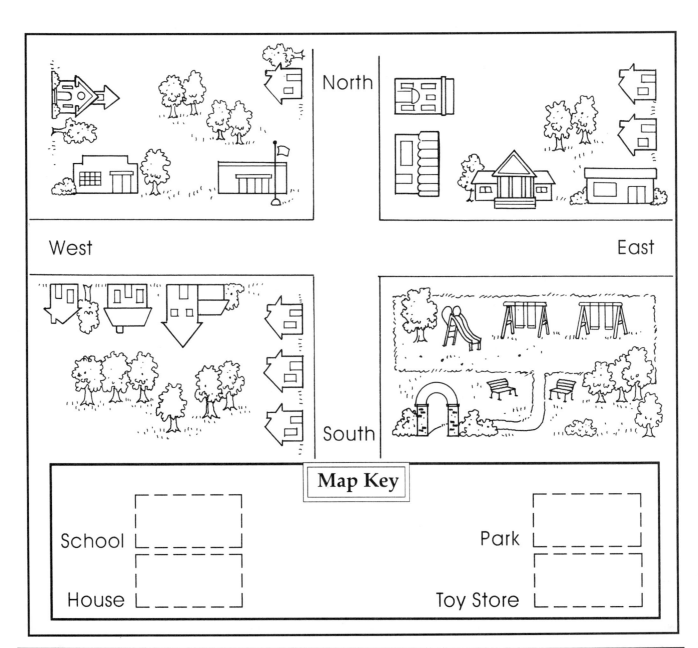

Name _____

A Venice Adventure

1. Start at the gondola, move 2 spaces south. Color the box blue.
2. Go east 2 spaces and draw a brown ⚓ anchor.
3. Go south 2 spaces and put an **X** in that box.
4. Move one space to the west and draw a red △ in that box.
5. Draw an 🛶 oar in the second box south of the △ .
6. Move 2 spaces east to get to the 🚢 dock at the finish.

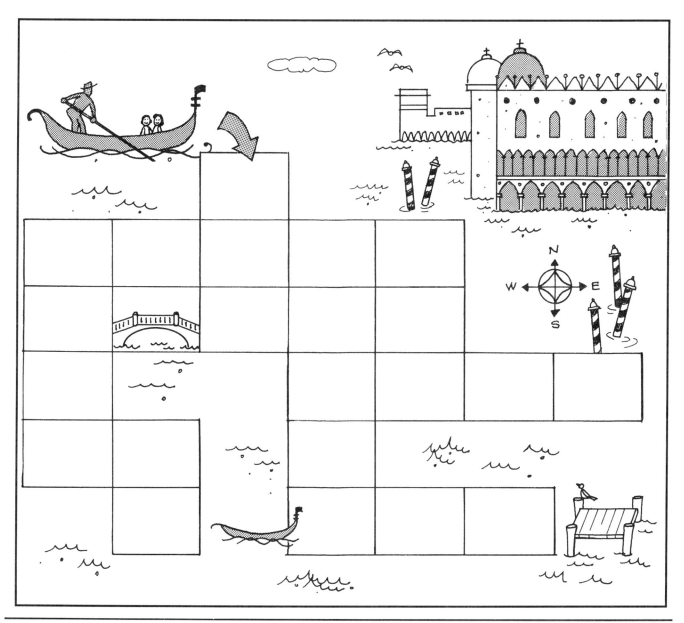

SOCIAL STUDIES

Name _____

Class Map

1. Add some symbols of your own to the map key.

2. Make a map of your classroom using the symbols found in the map key.

3. Add N, S, E, and W to your map.

Student's desk

Teacher's desk

_____

_____

Map Key

Name _____

Nick's Neighborhood

Draw a line along the path Nick used to get home.

1. Nick left the library and stopped to play on the school swings.

2. Next he looked at the puppies in the pet store window.

3. Nick watched as the fire truck raced out of the fire station.

4. Then Nick ran home to get money to buy an ice-cream cone.

SOCIAL STUDIES

Name _____

Cities, Towns, and Rural Areas

1. Cut and paste the correct signs on each picture.
2. Draw a door on the barn.
3. Draw another tall building in the city.
4. Color the PARK sign yellow.
5. Write where you live in the last picture.
6. Color the pictures.

Town

Rural Area

City

Name _____

Our State

1. Use a red crayon to outline your state.
2. Color the star yellow and the circle blue.
3. Cut and paste the star where the capital city is located.
4. Cut and paste the circle where your city is located.
5. Complete the sentences below.

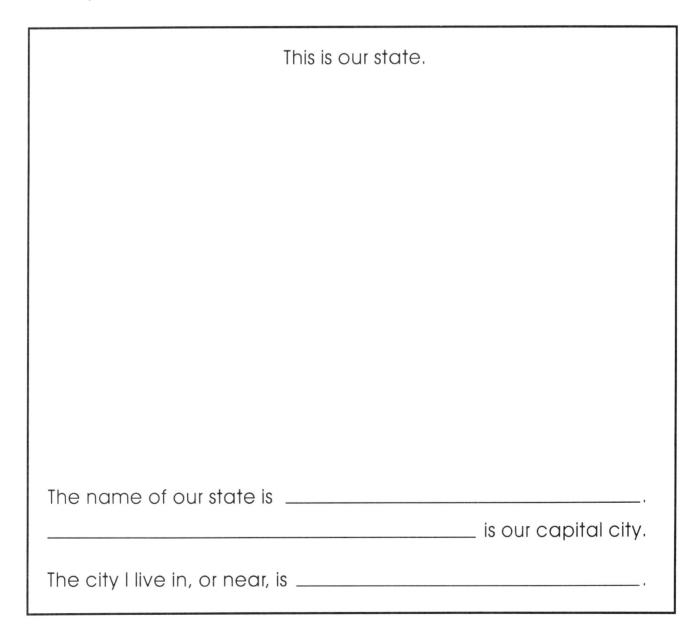

This is our state.

The name of our state is _____.

_____ is our capital city.

The city I live in, or near, is _____.

SOCIAL STUDIES

Name _____

Our Country

1. Outline the map green.

2. Color your state blue. Mark an **X** where you live.

3. Color the rest of the map yellow.

4. Trace the sentence at the bottom in black.

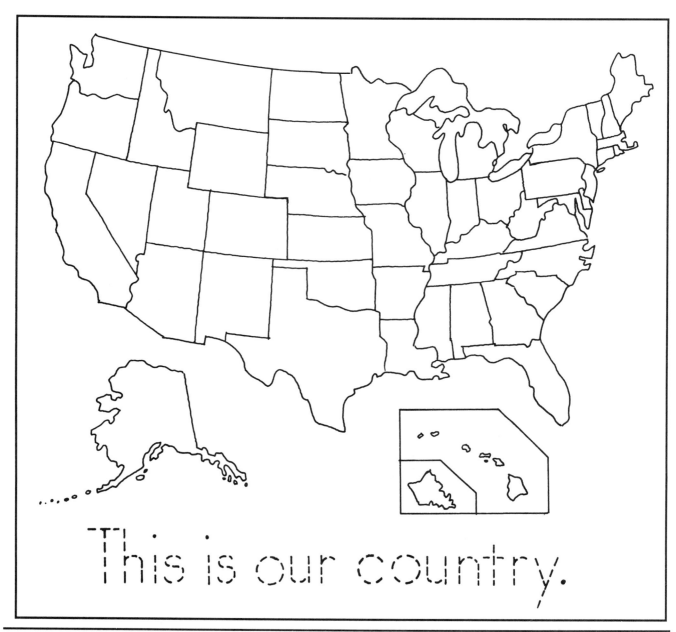

This is our country.

Scrambled Continents

Unscramble the words below to spell the continents correctly. Remember to cross out the letters you use. Put in capitals where needed. Use the word bank to help you.

1. rtonh miecara __ __ __ __ __   __ __ __ __ __ __ __

2. cfiara __ __ __ __ __ __

3. eropeu __ __ __ __ __ __

4. uhots ecaamir __ __ __ __ __ __   __ __ __ __ __ __ __

5. saia __ __ __ __

6. tnrtaiacac __ __ __ __ __ __ __ __ __ __

7. asurilaat __ __ __ __ __ __ __ __ __

| Africa | Australia | North America | Antarctica |
| Asia | Europe | South America | |

SOCIAL STUDIES

Name _____

Land Ho!

1. Draw a ◯ around the word mountains. Then color the mountains black.

2. Draw a ☐ around the word hills. Then color the hills green.

3. Draw a △ around the word plains. Then color the plains brown.

4. Put an **X** under the word water. Then color the water blue.

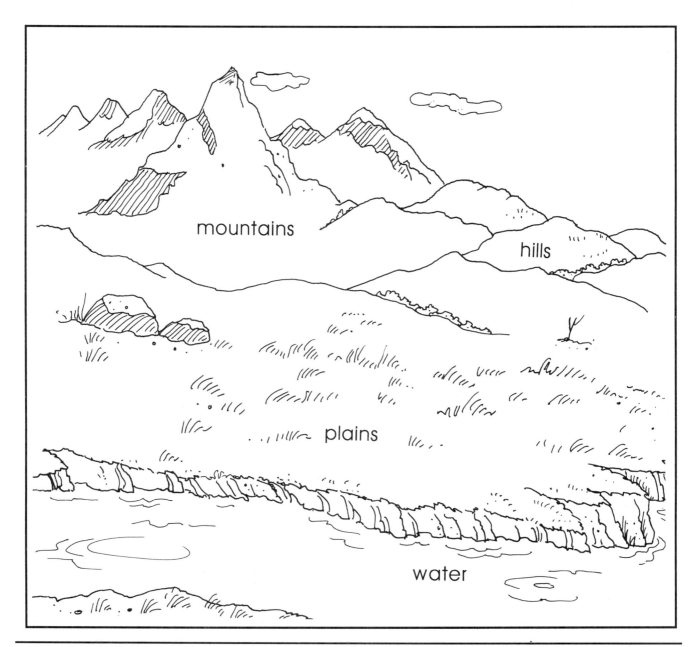

Name _____

Home Rules

1. Number the pictures in the correct order.
2. Then color the pictures.

Keep your room clean.

Be helpful.

Take care of the yard.

SOCIAL STUDIES

Name _____

School Rules

1. Draw a red circle around the good rules.
2. Draw a black **X** on the bad rules.
3. Then write one of your school rules.

Run in the halls.

Raise your hand in class.

Listen when your teacher talks.

Push friends when standing in line.

Talk anytime in class.

Walk in the halls.

Do not push friends when standing in line.

Fight with friends on the playground.

Be noisy in the library.

Be quiet in the library.

Quietly put school things away.

Stand up when riding the school bus.

Throw paper on the floor.

Clean up your lunch area.

One of our school rules is . . . _____

_____

Name _____

Traffic Signs and Signals

1. Color the STOP sign red.
2. Color the YIELD sign yellow.
3. Do NOT color the DO NOT ENTER sign.
4. Make the TRAFFIC LIGHT green.
5. Color the arrow on the ONE WAY sign black.
6. Color the WALK sign blue.

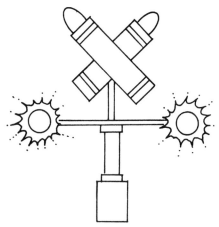

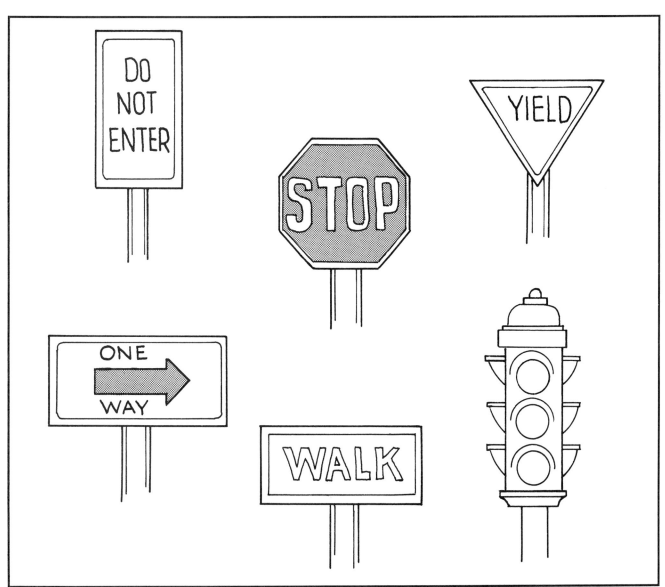

SOCIAL STUDIES

Name _____

Watch Out!

We should always obey safety rules.

1. Draw a black circle around five things that are wrong in the picture.
2. Then color the picture.

Name _____

Our State's Rules

1. Use the code to complete sentences 1, 2, and 3.

A	C	E	G	I	L	N
1	3	5	7	9	12	14

2. Then write your own answers for sentences 4 and 5.

O	P	R	S	T	V	W
15	16	18	19	20	22	23

1. State rules are called __ __ __ __ .
                 12 1 23 19

2. Laws are made in our state __ __ __ __ __ __ __ .
              3 1 16 9 20 1 12

3. The leader of our state is the __ __ __ __ __ __ __ __ .
              7 15 22 5 18 14 15 18

4. We live in the state of _____ .

5. The capital of our state is _____ .

SOCIAL STUDIES

IF8693 Super Book for Grade 1

Name _____

Our Nation's Laws

1. Use the Word Bank to write the answers for sentences 1, 2, and 3.

2. Write the name of our nation's President in sentence 4.

Word Bank

President

laws

Washington, D.C.

3. Draw a picture of our President inside the picture frame.

4. Color the frame and the picture.

1. Our nation's rules are called _____ .

2. The White House is in _____ .

3. Washington D.C. is where our _____ lives.

4. Our President's name is _____ .

Name _____

Native American Tribes

1. Color the Indian pictures and the different locations on the map.

2. Cut and paste the pictures correctly on the map.

  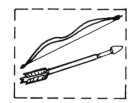  

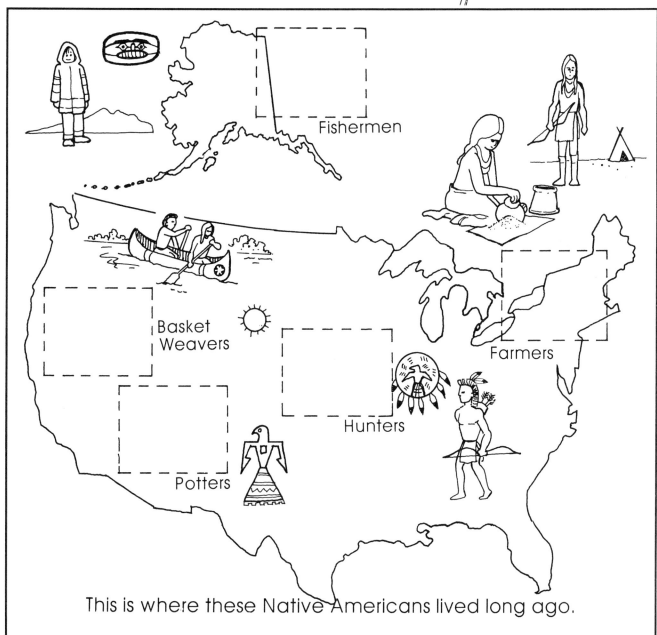

Fishermen

Basket
Weavers

Hunters

Farmers

Potters

This is where these Native Americans lived long ago.

SOCIAL STUDIES

Name _____

Native American Homes

1. Write teepee in box 1.

2. Write adobe in box 2.

3. Write wigwam in box 3.

4. Write longhouse in box 4.

5. Draw a sun on the teepee.

6. Color the longhouse brown.

7. Draw a door on the wigwam.

8. Draw small windows on the adobe.

1.

2.

3.

4.

Name _____

Native American Tools

1. Draw a red circle around the corn mortar and the salmon spear.
2. Draw a blue triangle around the digging stick and the fishhook.
3. Draw a green rectangle around the bow and arrow, the canoe paddle, and the hoe.
4. Draw a yellow square around the copper knife and the grinding stones.

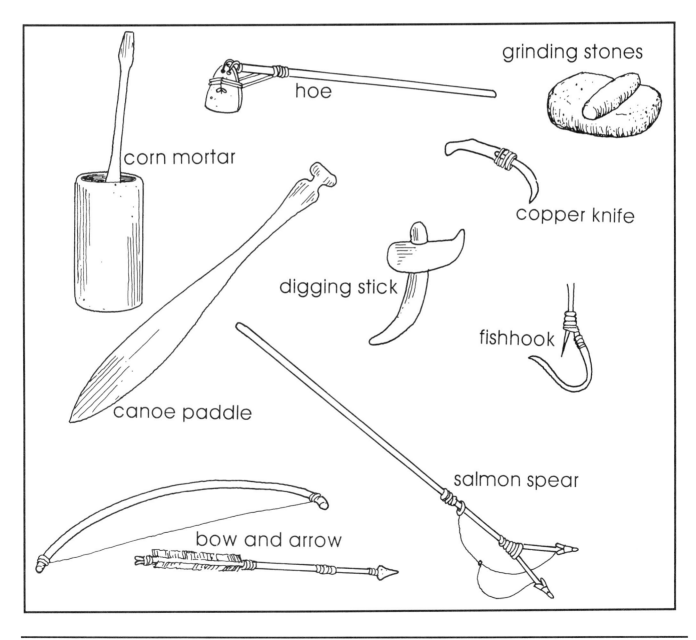

grinding stones

hoe

corn mortar

copper knife

digging stick

fishhook

canoe paddle

salmon spear

bow and arrow

SOCIAL STUDIES

Name _____

The First Thanksgiving

Help the pilgrims find food for their first Thanksgiving.

1. Draw a brown circle around each type of food from the Word Bank hidden in the picture below.

2. Then color the picture.

Word Bank	
corn	pumpkin
squash	turkey
onion	beans
berries	fish

A Whole New World

Name _____

Write each word on the line next to the matching picture.

| **Word Bank** | berries | corn | plant | Indian | ocean |
| | Pilgrim | ship | quail | forest | turkey |

SOCIAL STUDIES

Name _____

Colonial Workers

1. Draw  shoes in the window for the shoemaker.

2. Make some dough for the baker to use to make bread.

3. Put a hammer in the blacksmith's hand.

4. Draw a dress on the hanger for the dressmaker.

5. Draw a saddle for the saddlemaker.

6. Make sacks of flour and sugar for the storekeeper.

Name _____

Clara Barton

1. Color the  medicine bottle brown.

2. Draw a bandage on the man's leg.

3. Color the cross on the wagon red.

4. Color Clara Barton's bag black.

5. Now color the rest of the picture.

SOCIAL STUDIES

Name _____

Martin Luther King, Jr.

1. Color the W's black.

2. Color the X's blue.

3. Color the Y's brown

4. Color the Z's pink.

5. Color the V's green.

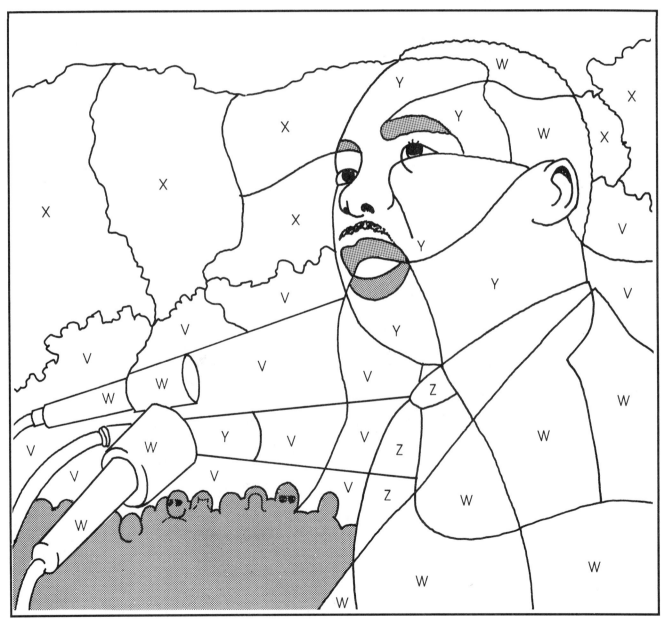

Name _____

Sally Ride

1. Color only the things Sally Ride would need in space.

2. Cut out and paste the colored pictures in the boxes below.

3. Then color Sally Ride.

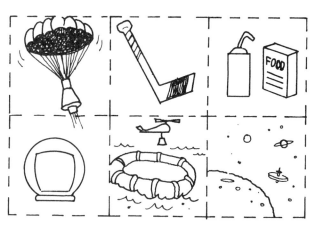

First Woman in Space – June 1983

SOCIAL STUDIES

Name _____

Person I Most Admire

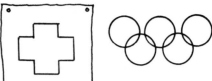

1. Think about the person you most admire.

2. Complete the sentences below.

3. Then draw a picture of yourself with that person.

The person I most admire is _____ .

I admire this person because _____

_____ .

Name _____

An African Aunt

1. Read each sentence and write the letter on the ant.

2. Then write each letter in order to find the answer to the riddle at the bottom.

1. Find the ninth letter in crocodile.

2. Write the first letter in lion.

3. What is the last letter in giraffe?

4. Find the middle letter in ape.

5. What letter is at the end of cheetah?

6. Write the fifth letter in zebra.

7. Find the last letter in python.

8. Write the third letter in ostrich.

What animal has the biggest aunt?

An __ __ __ __ __ __ __ __ __

SOCIAL STUDIES

Name _____

Chinese Challenge

Use the Word Bank to write the correct words in the sentences.

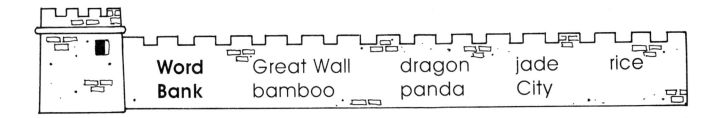

Word Bank   Great Wall   dragon   jade   rice
   bamboo   panda   City

1. It grows in China and rhymes with "can do."

   __ __ __ __ __ __
   1

2. Many Chinese stories are written about this monster.

   __ __ __ __ __ __
         7

3. A beautiful green stone.   __ __ __ __
                              4

4. This animal could once be found only in China.

   __ __ __ __ __
         6

5. Chinese Emperors once lived in the Forbidden __ __ __ __.
                                                    3

6. The long wall in China is called the

   __ __ __ __ __ __   __ __ __ __.
         2

7. A very important food in the Chinese diet is __ __ __ __.
                                                    5

   Write the numbered letters in order to find the name of this important city in China.

   __ __ __ __ __ __ __
   1   2   3   4   5   6   7

Answer Key

The Alphabet

a line to connect the dots. Follow the letters of the alphabet.

Page 1

Under-Cover Work

Color the pictures. Then cut them out and glue onto Ira's sleeping bag in ABC order.

Page 2

The Quail Trail

Read the words. Cut and paste them on the quails in alphabetical order.

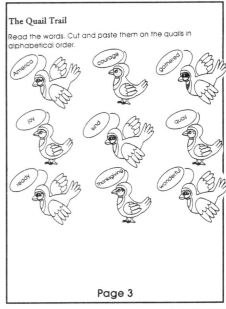

Page 3

Squeeze a Summer Sipper

Read the words on the juicer. Write them in alphabetical order.

Word Bank
school apples leaves
working playing blossoms
town clothes mowing

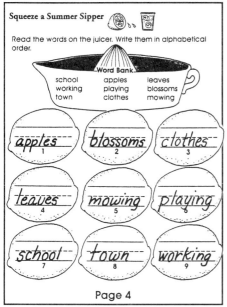

1. apples
2. blossoms
3. clothes
4. leaves
5. mowing
6. playing
7. school
8. town
9. working

Page 4

Morris Learns the Alphabet

To help Morris find his way to the candy store write the words from the Word Bank in ABC order.

Word Bank
desk time
bedtime climb
moose yelled
spell hid
numbers another

1. another
2. bedtime
3. climb
4. desk
5. hid
6. moose
7. numbers
8. spell
9. time
10. yelled

Page 5

Ghosts and Spaceships

Write the words in ABC order on the correct picture.

Color space word boxes red and blue.
Color Halloween word boxes orange and black.

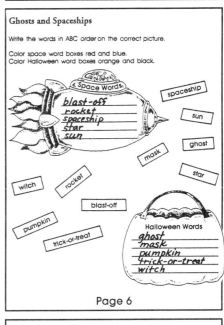

Space Words
blast-off
rocket
spaceship
star
sun

Halloween Words
ghost
mask
pumpkin
trick-or-treat
witch

Page 6

Alpha-bear-tical Antics

Follow the directions to answer the riddle below. In each paw, print the letter that comes...

1. Between H and J — I
2. After G — H
3. Before N — M
4. After A — B
5. Between S and U — T
6. Before S — R
7. After K — L
8. Before B — A
9. Between D and F — E

Now answer the riddle by writing the letter from each paw print in the space above the same number.

Riddle
What famous lady bear was the first to fly across the Atlantic Ocean?

A M E L I A
4 9 2 6 3 4

B E A R H A R T
9 2 8 1 5 8 6 5

Page 7

Letter Lift

Cut out the letter squares. Paste each square on the correct balloon.

Vowels: a e i o u o

Consonants: r s m n / v g t j / x p q h d / c k l b f

Page 8

"Feast" Your Eyes on This!

Look at the picture. Find and circle the letters that are hidden in the picture that spell **Happy Thanksgiving**. Color the picture.

Page 9

Sea Search

Help the boat sail to the island! Color the fish:
capital letters—orange   lower-case letters—blue

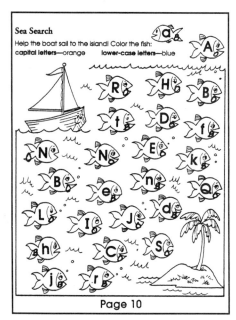

Page 10

Take One or Two

Look at each picture on the cookies and read the word below it. Cut and paste each cookie on the correct jar to show how many syllables are in the word.

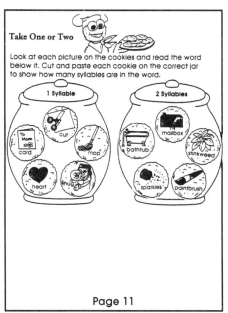

Page 11

Two for the Dragon

Cut out the muffins. Glue the six muffins with two-syllable words on the dragon's tummy. Glue the rest in the center of another sheet of drawing paper. Then create and color your own dragon around these muffins.

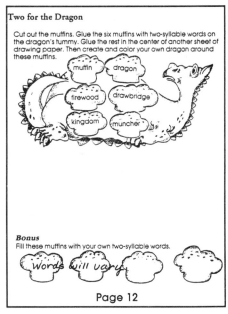

Bonus
Fill these muffins with your own two-syllable words.

Page 12

Half a Zoo

McGrew needs your help to capture the other half of these new zoo animals. Draw a matching half for each picture on this page and on the next. Color.

Page 13

Warm and Cozy

Look at the picture very carefully. All of the animals are snuggled in different places. Circle the eight animals hidden in the picture. Then color the picture.

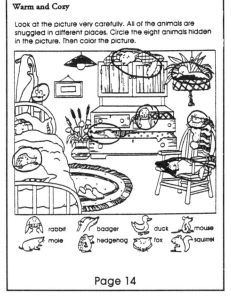

Page 14

Hidden Pebble Search

Sylvester hid 20 magic pebbles in this picture. Find the pebbles. Color them red and circle them with black. Then color the rest of the picture.

Page 15

Snowy Day

Circle the mistakes in this crazy, snowy-day picture. Then color all parts of the picture.

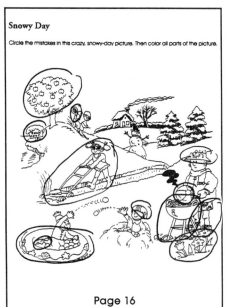

Page 16

Select a Synonym

Read the words. ✎ the word that means almost the same as the first word.

Page 17

Similar Meanings

Read the words in the word box. ✎ two words under each picture.

Page 18

A Change in the Weather

Change Alexander's cloudy day into a sunny day! Cut and paste an opposite in the ☀ for each ☁ word.

Page 19

Attach an Antonym

Read the word on each person. Find the word above the hair that means the opposite and paste it on that head.

Page 20

In or Out?

Read the words. Find a word in the Word Bank that means the opposite of each word given. Then write it on the line.

1. up   _down_
2. in   _out_
3. sad   _happy_
4. stop   _go_
5. big   _little_
6. on   _off_
7. left   _right_
8. here   _there_
9. yes   _no_
10. mother _father_

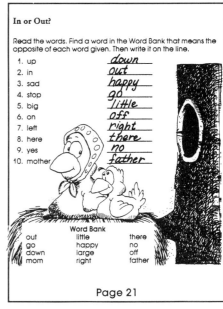

Word Bank

out	little	there
go	happy	no
down	large	off
mom	right	father

Page 21

Same or Opposite?

Color the spaces yellow that have word pairs with opposite meanings. Color the spaces blue that have word pairs with the same meanings.

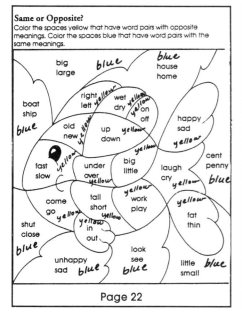

Page 22

Two Words in One

✏ the two words that make up each compound word below.

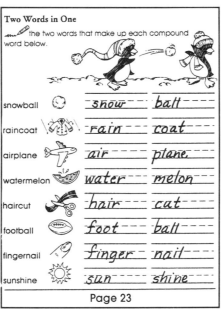

snowball — _snow_ — _ball_
raincoat — _rain_ — _coat_
airplane — _air_ — _plane_
watermelon — _water_ — _melon_
haircut — _hair_ — _cut_
football — _foot_ — _ball_
fingernail — _finger_ — _nail_
sunshine — _sun_ — _shine_

Page 23

It's Raining Meatballs!

Draw a line from each word in List A to a word in List B to make a compound word. On another piece of paper, write the compound words and draw pictures of them.

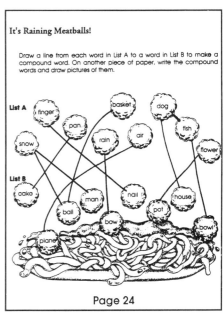

List A
List B

Page 24

"Compound"-ing the Cave's Echo

Read the words in the Word Bank. Find the two words that go together to make a compound word and write it on a bat.

bath	bed	bee
birth	by	comb
cow	day	every
fire	flies	for
got	grass	hide
hive	honey	lands
lights	near	one
spread	room	street

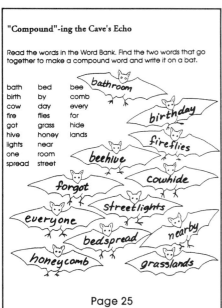

bathroom
birthday
fireflies
beehive
cowhide
forgot
streetlights
everyone
bedspread
nearby
honeycomb
grasslands

Page 25

Let's Make a Snowman

✏ a line from each pair of words to the right contraction.

he is — it's
it is — she's
she is — he's
they are — you're
you are — they're
we are — I'm
I am — we're

Page 26

Loppy Ears

A contraction is a short way to write two words. Choose a contraction from the big carrot and print it on the lines.

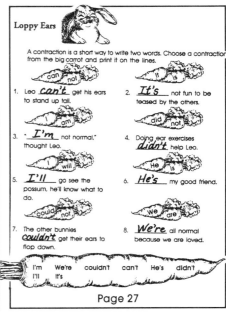

1. Leo _can't_ get his ears to stand up tall.
2. _It's_ not fun to be teased by the others.
3. "_I'm_ not normal," thought Leo.
4. Doing ear exercises _didn't_ help Leo.
5. _I'll_ go see the possum, he'll know what to do.
6. _He's_ my good friend.
7. The other bunnies _couldn't_ get their ears to flop down.
8. _We're_ all normal because we are loved.

I'm   We're   couldn't   can't   He's   didn't   I'll   It's

Page 27

IF8693 Super Book for Grade 1

"Crumb"-y Contractions

Read the two words on the bread crumbs. Find the contraction in the Word Bank and write it on the bird.

we're — we / are
that's — that / is
I'd — I / would
I'll — will
she's — she / is
they're — they / are
she'd — she / would
let's — let / us
we'd — we / would

Word Bank:
we'd   she's
let's   I'll
I'd   we're
         they're
         that's
         she'd

Page 28

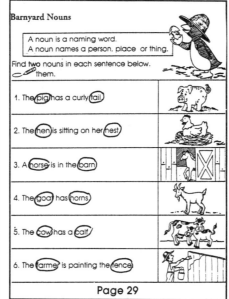

Barnyard Nouns

A noun is a naming word.
A noun names a person, place or thing.

Find two nouns in each sentence below. ✏ them.

1. The pig has a curly tail.
2. The hen is sitting on her nest.
3. A horse is in the barn.
4. The goat has horns.
5. The cow has a calf.
6. The farmer is painting the fence.

Page 29

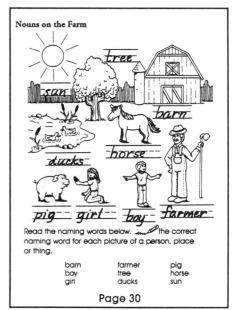

Nouns on the Farm

sun   tree   barn   ducks   horse   pig   girl   boy   farmer

Read the naming words below. ✏ the correct naming word for each picture of a person, place or thing.

barn   farmer   pig
boy   tree   horse
girl   ducks   sun

Page 30

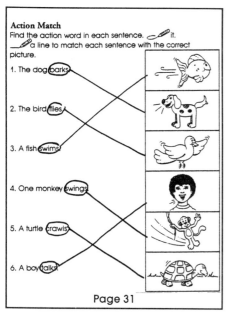

Action Match

Find the action word in each sentence. ✏ it.
✏ a line to match each sentence with the correct picture.

1. The dog barks.
2. The bird flies.
3. A fish swims.
4. One monkey swings.
5. A turtle crawls.
6. A boy talks.

Page 31

Circus Action

A verb is an action word. A verb tells what a person or thing does or did.

Find the verb in each sentence below and ✏ it.

1. The bear climbs a ladder.
2. Two tiny dogs dance.
3. A boy eats cotton candy.
4. A woman swings on a trapeze.
5. The clown falls down.
6. A tiger jumps through a ring.

Page 32

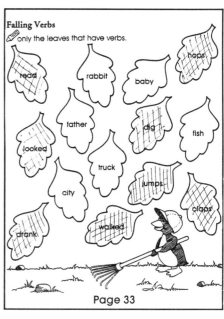

Falling Verbs

✏ only the leaves that have verbs.

read   rabbit   baby   hops
father   dig   fish
looked
truck
city   jumps
drank   walked   claps

Page 33

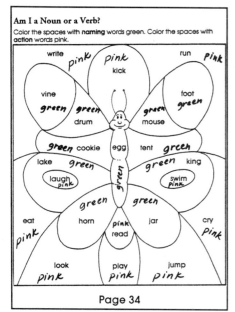

Am I a Noun or a Verb?

Color the spaces with **naming** words green. Color the spaces with **action** words pink.

write   pink   pink   run   pink
kick
vine   green   green   foot   green
drum   mouse
green   cookie   egg   tent   green
lake   green   green   king
laugh   swim
pink   pink
green   green
eat   horn   pink   jar   cry
pink   read   pink
look   play   jump
pink   pink   pink

Page 34

Animal Adjectives

✏ a describing word in each sentence below.
Use the word bank to help you.

Word Bank
big   bushy   three
round   green   six

1. A ___ has a _bushy_ tail.
2. A ___ has _six_ legs.
3. The ___ will become a _green_ frog.
4. A ___ has _big_ teeth.
5. _Three_ ___ hang by their tails.
6. An ___ has _round_ eyes.

Page 35

Fishing for Adjectives

✏ only the fish with describing words.

rug
bushy
fluffy   pig
bed
warm
moon
quilt

Page 36

Corn Crackles

Here are some describing words:

sour   furry   sweet   tasty   crisp
tall   crunchy   cloudy   sad   soft

Which four words do you think might best describe the cereal? Write them on the lines on the cereal box.

crunchy
sweet
tasty
crisp

Page 37

The Turtles Tell

Some sentences tell something.
Telling sentences begin with a capital letter.
Telling sentences end with a period.

Circle only the sentences that tell.

1. Two turtles sat on a log.
2. One turtle fell off.
3. Did you see him?
4. He swam away.
5. The water is cold.
6. Can you swim?

Page 38

All About Dinosaurs

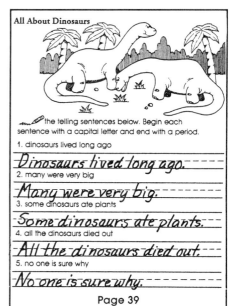

Write the telling sentences below. Begin each sentence with a capital letter and end with a period.

1. dinosaurs lived long ago

Dinosaurs lived long ago.

2. many were very big

Many were very big.

3. some dinosaurs ate plants

Some dinosaurs ate plants.

4. all the dinosaurs died out

All the dinosaurs died out.

5. no one is sure why

No one is sure why.

Page 39

State It!

Some sentences tell something. They are called statements. A statement begins with a capital letter and ends with a period.

Write these statements correctly.

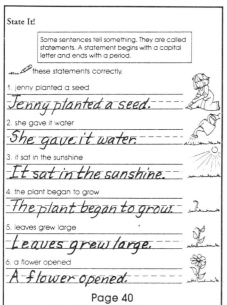

1. jenny planted a seed

Jenny planted a seed.

2. she gave it water

She gave it water.

3. it sat in the sunshine

It sat in the sunshine.

4. the plant began to grow

The plant began to grow.

5. leaves grew large

Leaves grew large.

6. a flower opened

A flower opened.

Page 40

Fishy Questions

Write the first word of each question below. Remember to begin with a capital letter. End each question with a question mark.

1. *Is* (is) that your boat?
2. *Did* (did) you catch that fish?
3. *How* (how) much does it weigh?
4. *Will* (will) you eat it?
5. *Did* (did) you fish with worms?
6. *Is* (is) the water cold?

Page 41

Did You Ask Me Something?

Some sentences ask something. They are called questions. A question begins with a capital letter and ends with a question mark.

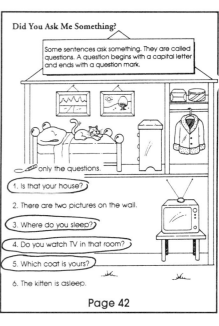

Circle only the questions.

1. Is that your house?
2. There are two pictures on the wall.
3. Where do you sleep?
4. Do you watch TV in that room?
5. Which coat is yours?
6. The kitten is asleep.

Page 42

Period or Question Mark?

Put a period or a question mark at the end of each sentence.

1. Can the fish jump out of the tank ?
2. Two snakes are in that cage .
3. How much does that turtle cost ?
4. Yes, I already have a dog .
5. His name is King .
6. Do you have a dog ?

Page 43

What a Trick!

If the word names an animal, color the space brown.
If the word names something to eat, color the space blue.
If the word names something found in the sky, color the space yellow.
If the word names a piece of furniture, color the space red.
If the word names something you use in school, color the space green.

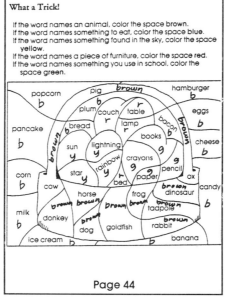

Page 44

Pick a Pouch

Cut and paste each word on the correct kangaroo pouch. Then color one kangaroo green and the other your favorite color.

Animal Words: cat, dog, bear, fish
Color Words: purple, red, blue, green

Page 45

"Cap" the Words

Read the headings on the caps. Write the words from the Word Bank on the correct cap.

How Clothes Can Feel
- warm
- itchy
- stiff
- hot

Words That Tell Where
- under
- over
- in
- on

Which word is left over? jacket

Word Bank
under   over   hot
warm   itchy   in
jacket   stiff   on

Page 46

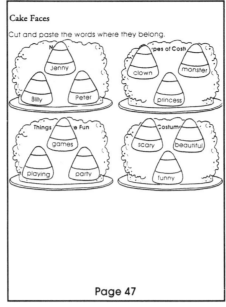

Cake Faces

Cut and paste the words where they belong.

Jenny   Billy   Peter

clown   monster   princess

games   playing   party

scary   beautiful   funny

Page 47

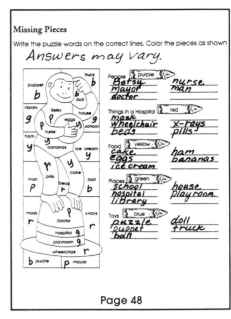

Missing Pieces

Write the puzzle words on the correct lines. Color the pieces as shown

Answers may vary.

People
- Betsy
- mayor
- doctor

- nurse
- man

Things in a Hospital
- mask
- wheelchair
- beds

- x-rays
- pills

Food
- cake
- eggs
- ice cream

- ham
- bananas

Places
- school
- hospital
- library

- house
- playroom

Toys
- puzzle
- puppet
- ball

- doll
- truck

Page 48

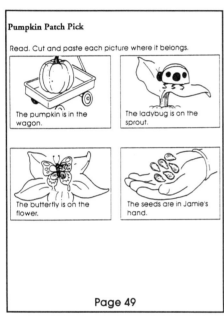

Pumpkin Patch Pick

Read. Cut and paste each picture where it belongs.

The pumpkin is in the wagon.

The ladybug is on the sprout.

The butterfly is on the flower.

The seeds are in Jamie's hand.

Page 49

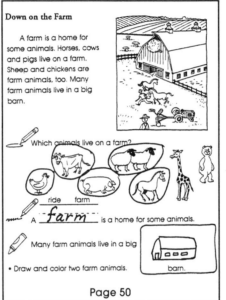

Down on the Farm

A farm is a home for some animals. Horses, cows and pigs live on a farm. Sheep and chickens are farm animals, too. Many farm animals live in a big barn.

Which animals live on a farm?

ride   farm
A farm is a home for some animals.

Many farm animals live in a big barn.

• Draw and color two farm animals.

Page 50

My Pet

It is fun to have a pet. Dogs and cats are good pets. Birds and rabbits can be pets, too. Pets are good friends. They need care and love every day.

friends   fast
Pets are good friends

Pets need care and love.

dog   rabbit   cat   bird

dog   bird
cat   rabbit

• Draw and color a picture of your pet.

Page 51

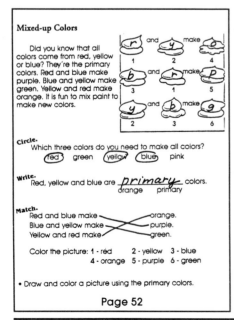

Mixed-up Colors

Did you know that all colors come from red, yellow or blue? They're the primary colors. Red and blue make purple. Blue and yellow make green. Yellow and red make orange. It is fun to mix paint to make new colors.

r and y make o
1   2   4

b and r make p
3   1   5

y and b make g
2   3   6

Circle.
Which three colors do you need to make all colors?
(red)   green   (yellow)   (blue)   pink

Write.
Red, yellow and blue are primary colors.
orange   primary

Match.
Red and blue make — orange.
Blue and yellow make — purple.
Yellow and red make — green.

Color the picture: 1 - red   2 - yellow   3 - blue
4 - orange   5 - purple   6 - green

• Draw and color a picture using the primary colors.

Page 52

Scrambled Shoes

Minnie needs new shoes. She tries on several pairs and decides on one pair. Oops! While trying on all of the shoes, she has scattered them all over. Now she can't find the other shoe of the pair she wants.

Help Minnie find her shoe. Using a different color for each pair of shoes, color each pair exactly the same. Then draw a circle around Minnie's missing shoe.

Page 53

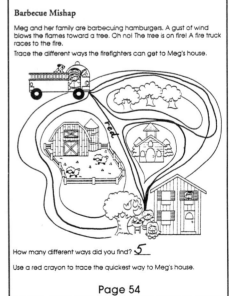

Barbecue Mishap

Meg and her family are barbecuing hamburgers. A gust of wind blows the flames toward a tree. Oh no! The tree is on fire! A fire truck races to the fire.

Trace the different ways the firefighters can get to Meg's house.

How many different ways did you find? 5

Use a red crayon to trace the quickest way to Meg's house.

Page 54

Musician's Choice

Many different instruments are used to make music. Irene knows how to play several musical instruments.

Irene knows how to play these instruments.

Irene does not know how to play these instruments.

Draw a circle around the instruments Irene probably also knows how to play.

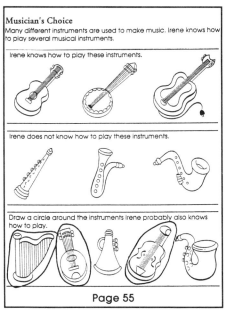

Page 55

Family Portraits

Families may be big or small. No matter how many people are in a family, each person is important to the others.

Cut out the pictures at the bottom of the page. Read the clues. Paste the pictures of the members of this family in the frame where they belong.

- Grandfather is in the middle.
- The girl is on the right end.
- The boy is on the left end.
- Mother is between Grandmother and the boy.
- Father is beside the girl.
- The family dog is between Grandfather and Father.

Page 56

Where Is That Sheep?

Read. Cut and paste each sheep where it belongs. Color the pictures.

The sheep is on the table.

The sheep is under the loom.

The sheep is in the pokeweed berry bush.

The sheep is beside the cloth.

The sheep is on Charlie's hat.

The sheep is in between the pieces of Charlie's cloak.

Page 57

Umbrellas Up!

Look at the pictures. Circle the correct word and write it on the line.

Molly puts __up__ the umbrella.
(up) on in

The tie is __on__ the bed.
up (on) in

The cat is __in__ the house.
up on (in)

The bird flies __up.__
up on in

He puts __on__ mittens.
up (on) in

The dog is __in__ the rain.
up on (in)

Page 58

Playing Parts

Look at each picture. Find the title of the story that Grace is acting out in the Word Bank. Write it under the correct picture.

Space Adventures

Cowboy Jake & the Roundup

The Lost Treasure Chest

The Case of the Missing Cat

Word Bank

The Case of the Missing Cat
Space Adventures
Cowboy Jake & the Roundup
The Lost Treasure Chest

Page 59

It's Time to . . .

Cut and paste four sentences under the correct pictures.

Susie's alarm clock rings.

Susie picks up her books.

It's time to get up.

It's time to go to school.

Susie is getting hungry.

Susie hears the school bell ring.

It's time to eat lunch.

It's time to go home from school.

Page 60

What Will They Do?

Read each sentence and question. Put a ✓ in the box by the correct answer. Draw a picture to answer the question.

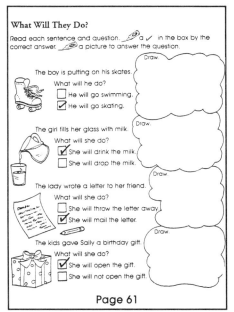

The boy is putting on his skates.
What will he do?
☐ He will go swimming.
☑ He will go skating.

The girl fills her glass with milk.
What will she do?
☑ She will drink the milk.
☐ She will drop the milk.

The lady wrote a letter to her friend.
What will she do?
☐ She will throw the letter away.
☑ She will mail the letter.

The kids gave Sally a birthday gift.
What will she do?
☑ She will open the gift.
☐ She will not open the gift.

Page 61

What Does That Mean?

Read. Color the picture that shows what each sentence really means.

We are just horsing around.

She had a puzzled look.

Pipe down, please.

He is down in the dumps.

The window flew open.

Page 62

Save Six

Color six animals.

Any six.

Color six things that will grow.

Draw pictures of six of your favorite things on the back of this paper.

Page 63

Where's the Hair?

Draw different kinds of hair on each head. Color.

Pictures will vary.

Page 64

Suited for Winter

Read and do.

1. Draw a hat on the snowman. Color the hat **purple** and **orange**.
2. Draw a snowsuit on the snowman. Color the snowsuit **blue**.
3. Draw boots on the snowman. Color the boots **yellow**.
4. Draw mittens on the snowman. Color the mittens **green**.

Page 65

Meet the Alien

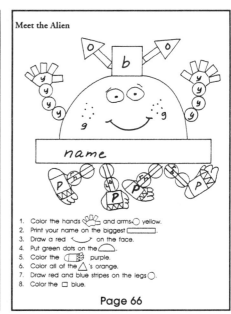

1. Color the hands and arms yellow.
2. Print your name on the biggest ▭.
3. Draw a red ⌣ on the face.
4. Put green dots on the ⌒.
5. Color the ▯ purple.
6. Color all of the △'s orange.
7. Draw red and blue stripes on the legs ◯.
8. Color the ▢ blue.

Page 66

What's the Idea?

Read the sentence in each speech bubble. Underline the main idea.

Page 67

Yes or No?

Read each sentence. Circle **yes** if the sentence tells about the picture. Circle **no** if it does not.

Page 68

Picture Pick

Look at each picture. Read the sentences. ✎ the correct letter in each ◯ to tell the main idea.

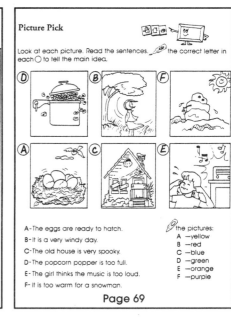

A-The eggs are ready to hatch.
B-It is a very windy day.
C-The old house is very spooky.
D-The popcorn popper is too full.
E-The girl thinks the music is too loud.
F-It is too warm for a snowman.

✎ the pictures:
A —yellow
B —red
C —blue
D —green
E —orange
F —purple

Page 69

What About Bear?

Read each sentence. Circle **yes** if the sentence tells about the picture. Circle **no** if it does not.

Page 70

What Did Morris Do Now?

Look at the pictures. Find the sentence in the Word Bank that matches each picture. Write it on the line.

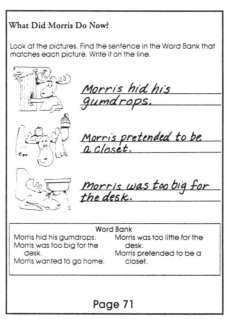

Morris hid his gumdrops.

Morris pretended to be a closet.

Morris was too big for the desk.

Word Bank
Morris hid his gumdrops.   Morris was too little for the
Morris was too big for the   desk.
desk.   Morris pretended to be a
Morris wanted to go home.   closet.

Page 71

What a Life!

Read each sentence. If it tells something that could really happen, paste it under the real dog. If it tells something that is make-believe, paste it under the make-believe dog.

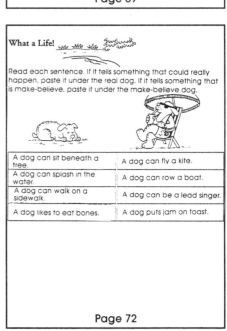

A dog can sit beneath a tree.	A dog can fly a kite.
A dog can splash in the water.	A dog can row a boat.
A dog can walk on a sidewalk.	A dog can be a lead singer.
A dog likes to eat bones.	A dog puts jam on toast.

Page 72

My Friend the Bear

Read each sentence. If it tells something that could really happen, color the real bear. If it tells something that is make-believe, color the toy bear.

Real Make-Believe

1. A bear can live in a forest. ✓
2. A bear can search in a store for a lost button. ✓
3. A girl can sew a button on a pair of overalls. ✓
4. A bear can talk to a little girl. ✓
5. A toy bear can ride up an escalator by himself. ✓
6. A toy bear can sit on a toy department shelf. ✓
7. A little girl can save money in a piggy bank. ✓
8. A toy bear and a little girl can be friends. ✓ or ✓
9. A toy bear can yank a button off a mattress. ✓

Page 73

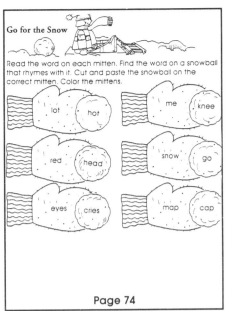

Go for the Snow

Read the word on each mitten. Find the word on a snowball that rhymes with it. Cut and paste the snowball on the correct mitten. Color the mittens.

lot hot   me knee

red head   snow go

eyes cries   map cap

Page 74

Strawberry Patch Match

Read the word on each strawberry. Find the word in the Word Bank that rhymes. Write it on the line.

sun — fan	Sam — jam
sky — high	day — away
bark — park	goat — boat
kite — might	tea — tree
flowers — showers	cool — school

Word Bank

away	boat	high	fun
might	park	tree	jam
showers	school		

Page 75

A Space Case!

Read the word on each spaceship. Find the words in the Word Bank that rhyme and write them on the line.

two — boo   small — tall   most — ghost
rock — knock   spotted — dotted door — four
cat — fat   me — three   funny — bunny
                               brown — clown

Word Bank

fat	ghost	patch
tall	knock	clown
boo	three	dotted
step	four	bunny

Page 76

Carrot Crop

Color the four pictures. Cut and paste the pictures in 1, 2, 3, 4 order.

Page 77

Fall Pick Up

Color the pictures. Cut and paste each picture in 1, 2, 3, 4 order.

Page 78

It's Hard to Wait!

Write 1, 2, 3, or 4 in the boot next to the picture to show the order it happened in the story. Then draw a line from the boot to the sentence that tells about that picture.

1 — He has a new snowsuit.
4 — He made a snowball.
2 — He put on his new snowsuit, boots, hat and mittens.
3 — He wished and wished for snow.

Page 79

How Many?

Read the words in the Word Bank. If the word means one, write it under Buster. If the word means more than one, write it under Sue Ellen.

one
1. straw
2. child
3. person
4. class
5. recess
6. tooth

more than one
1. teeth
2. babies
3. men
4. children
5. people
6. patients

Word Bank

teeth	child	class	people
straw	men	children	tooth
babies	person	recess	patients

Page 80

Animal Chatter

Unscramble the letters and write the name of each animal. Color the correct animal sound in each.

squeak   baa   gobble   moo   quack   meow   roar

oiln — lion   emuos — mouse   cdku — duck
pehse — sheep   ekyurt — turkey
wco — cow   tnitke — kitten

roar / quack / squeak / baa / gobble / moo / meow

Page 81

IF8693 Super Book for Grade 1

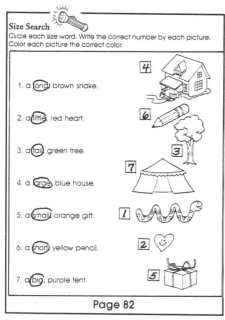

Size Search
Circle each size word. Write the correct number by each picture.
Color each picture the correct color.

1. a long, brown snake. 4
2. a little, red heart. 6
3. a tall, green tree. 3
4. a large, blue house. 7
5. a small, orange gift. 1
6. a short, yellow pencil. 2
7. a big, purple tent. 5

Page 82

Confection Perfection
Cut out the pictures of the candy at the bottom of the page. Paste the pictures to correctly continue the pattern in each row.

Page 83

Roaring Roller-Coaster Rides
Cut out the roller coaster cars at the bottom of the page. Paste them to correctly continue the pattern on each track.

Page 84

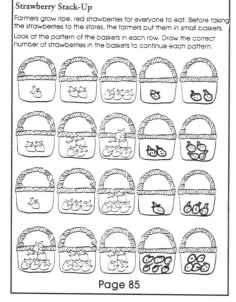

Strawberry Stack-Up
Farmers grow ripe, red strawberries for everyone to eat. Before taking the strawberries to the stores, the farmers put them in small baskets.
Look at the pattern of the baskets in each row. Draw the correct number of strawberries in the baskets to continue each pattern.

Page 85

Stringing It Along
Complete each pattern. Color the ♡ red and the ♡ pink.

Page 86

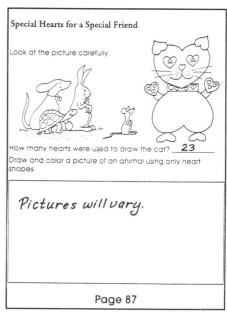

Special Hearts for a Special Friend
Look at the picture carefully.

How many hearts were used to draw the cat? __23__
Draw and color a picture of an animal using only heart shapes.

Pictures will vary.

Page 87

Animal Action
Find the shapes and color the picture using the code.

○ red   ☐ blue   ▭ yellow
△ green   ◇ orange   ⬭ black

Page 88

Cabin to Capitol
Abraham Lincoln was the 16th president of the United States. He was born in a log cabin. Many people lived in log cabins at that time.
Look at this picture of a log cabin. How many of each of the different shapes can you find in the picture?

How many △'s? _3_   How many ▱'s? _6_
How many ☐'s? _9_   Draw and color a door.

Page 89

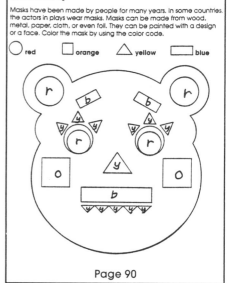

Mask Make-Up
Masks have been made by people for many years. In some countries, the actors in plays wear masks. Masks can be made from wood, metal, paper, cloth, or even foil. They can be painted with a design or a face. Color the mask by using the color code.

○ red   ☐ orange   △ yellow   ▭ blue

Page 90

Animal Shapes

Color:
squares ——— green
rectangles ——— yellow
circles ——— red
triangles ——— blue

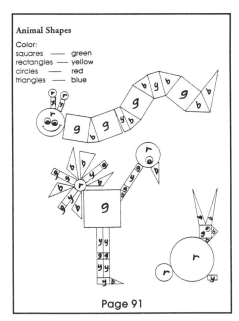

Page 91

"Squaring" Off

Square dancing is a kind of folk dancing. The name of the dance comes from the shape the group of dancers form when they begin the dance – a square. As they dance, they form other shapes.

Look at the shapes and answer the questions.

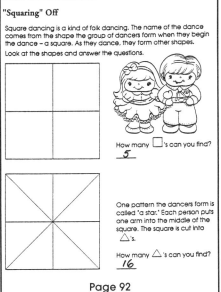

How many ☐'s can you find?
5

One pattern the dancers form is called "a star." Each person puts one arm into the middle of the square. The square is cut into △'s.

How many △'s can you find?
16

Page 92

Rainbow-Colored Numbers

Color: 1's—red
2's—blue
3's—yellow
4's—green
5's—orange

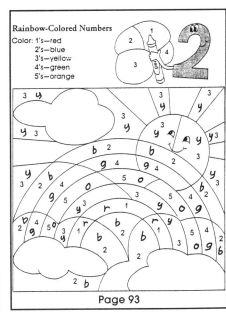

Page 93

One Beautiful Butterfly

Color: 6's—purple
7's—yellow
8's—black
9's—orange
10's—brown

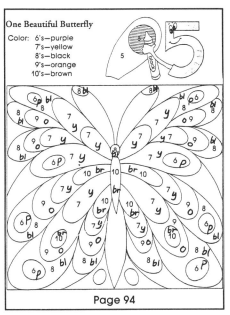

Page 94

Clown Count

Color the balloon's:

1 - blue   2 - orange   3 - yellow   4 - green
5 - purple   6 - brown
7 - red   8 - black   9 - blue   10 - purple

Color clown, too!

Page 95

Wintry Ride

Count each set of bears. Draw a line from each set to the sled that has the correct number.

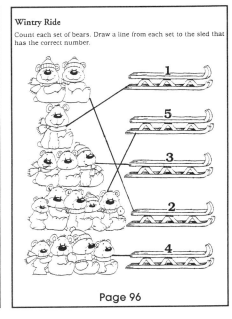

Page 96

Pack a Snack

Count each set of sandwiches. Draw a line from each set to the backpack that has the correct number.

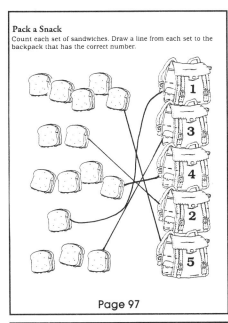

Page 97

Sheepish Shepherd

Count the sheep on each hill. Then write that number on each tree.

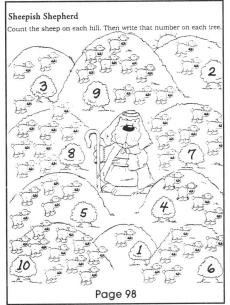

Page 98

Number Express

Number the train.

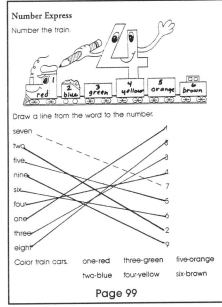

Draw a line from the word to the number.

seven
two
five
nine
six
four
one
three
eight

Color train cars.   one-red   three-green   five-orange
two-blue   four-yellow   six-brown

Page 99

Beach Blanket Numbers
Count. Use code to color answers.

1—blue 4—red 7—purple
2—yellow 5—orange 8—gray
3—green 6—brown 9—black

Page 100

School Scene

How many?

Page 101

Take an Animal Count!
Count the zoo animals in each box. Match the number to the correct number word by drawing a line to it. One is done for you.

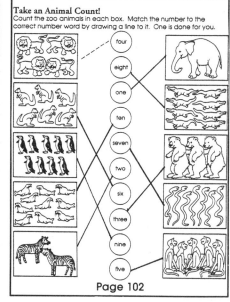

Page 102

Connect the Dots
Join the dots in order.
Color the surprise.

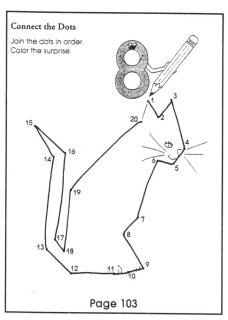

Page 103

More Dot-to-Dot Fun

Connect the dots.

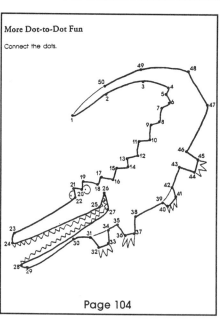

Page 104

Happy Hikers
Hike your way to camp. Trace a path through the maze by counting from 1 to 10 in the correct order. Color the picture.

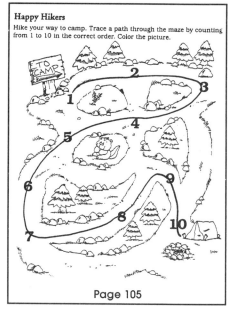

Page 105

Two for the Pool
Counting by 2's, write the numbers to 50 in the waterdrops. Start at the top of the slide and go down.

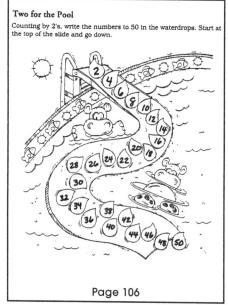

Page 106

I'm Counting on You
Write and count by 2's.

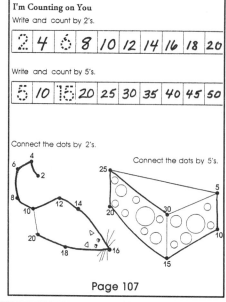

Write and count by 5's.

Connect the dots by 2's.

Connect the dots by 5's.

Page 107

Count the Cookie Clues
Find out what holds something crumbly, but good! Counting by 5's, connect the dots in order. Start with 5. Color the picture.

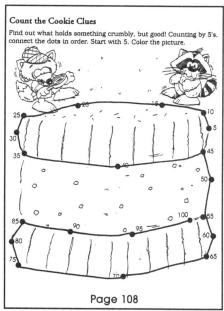

Page 108

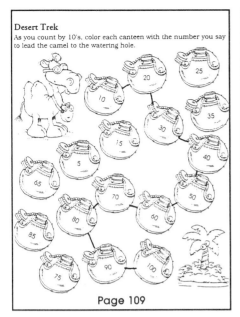

Desert Trek

As you count by 10's, color each canteen with the number you say to lead the camel to the watering hole.

Page 109

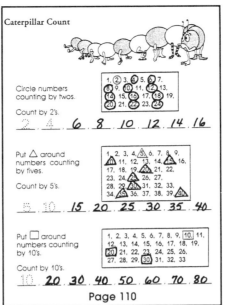

Caterpillar Count

Circle numbers counting by twos.

Count by 2's.

2, 4, 6, 8, 10, 12, 14, 16

Put △ around numbers counting by fives.

Count by 5's.

5, 10, 15, 20, 25, 30, 35, 40

Put ☐ around numbers counting by 10's.

Count by 10's.

10, 20, 30, 40, 50, 60, 70, 80

Page 110

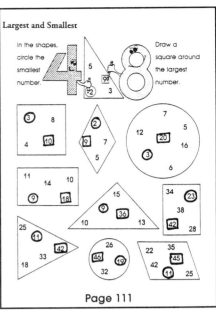

Largest and Smallest

In the shapes, circle the smallest number.

Draw a square around the largest number.

Page 111

Barking Up a Tree

Use counters. Trace or draw each set you make. Then, write how many in all.

How many?	How many more?	How many in all?
3	2	5
2	1	3
4	3	7
1	6	7

Think of a story for this picture. Write how many in all.

5 in all

Page 112

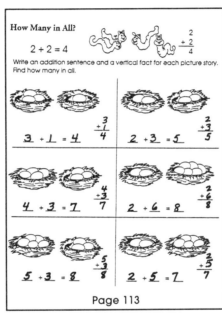

How Many in All?

$2 + 2 = 4$ $\begin{array}{r}2\\+2\\\hline 4\end{array}$

Write an addition sentence and a vertical fact for each picture story. Find how many in all.

$3 + 1 = 4$ $\begin{array}{r}3\\+1\\\hline 4\end{array}$

$2 + 3 = 5$ $\begin{array}{r}2\\+3\\\hline 5\end{array}$

$4 + 3 = 7$ $\begin{array}{r}4\\+3\\\hline 7\end{array}$

$2 + 6 = 8$ $\begin{array}{r}2\\+6\\\hline 8\end{array}$

$5 + 3 = 8$ $\begin{array}{r}5\\+3\\\hline 8\end{array}$

$2 + 5 = 7$ $\begin{array}{r}2\\+5\\\hline 7\end{array}$

Page 113

Addition Using Counters

Example $2 + 1 = ?$

Use counters to add.

Put in 2.   Put in 1 more.

How many counters are there in all? 3

So, $2 + 1 = 3$. The number that tells how many in all is called the **sum**. The sum of 2 + 1 is 3.

Use counters to find each sum.

$2 + 4 = 6$ $5 + 2 = 7$

$3 + 3 = 6$ $3 + 4 = 7$

Page 114

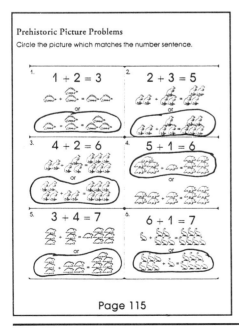

Prehistoric Picture Problems

Circle the picture which matches the number sentence.

1. $1 + 2 = 3$ 2. $2 + 3 = 5$

3. $4 + 2 = 6$ 4. $5 + 1 = 6$

5. $3 + 4 = 7$ 6. $6 + 1 = 7$

Page 115

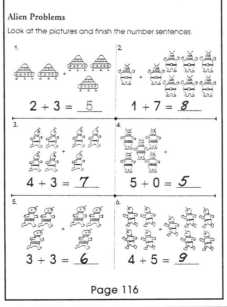

Alien Problems

Look at the pictures and finish the number sentences.

1. $2 + 3 = 5$ 2. $1 + 7 = 8$

3. $4 + 3 = 7$ 4. $5 + 0 = 5$

5. $3 + 3 = 6$ 6. $4 + 5 = 9$

Page 116

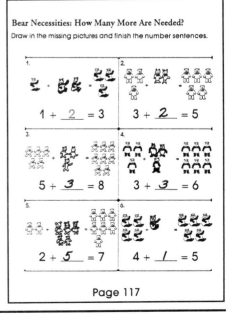

Bear Necessities: How Many More Are Needed?

Draw in the missing pictures and finish the number sentences.

1. $1 + 2 = 3$ 2. $3 + 2 = 5$

3. $5 + 3 = 8$ 4. $3 + 3 = 6$

5. $2 + 5 = 7$ 6. $4 + 1 = 5$

Page 117

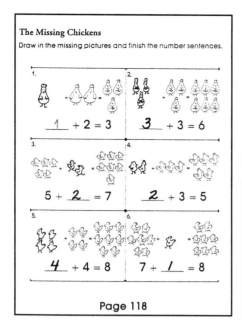

The Missing Chickens
Draw in the missing pictures and finish the number sentences.

1. __4__ + 2 = 3
2. __3__ + 3 = 6
3. 5 + __2__ = 7
4. __2__ + 3 = 5
5. __4__ + 4 = 8
6. 7 + __1__ = 8

Page 118

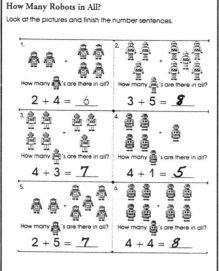

How Many Robots in All?
Look at the pictures and finish the number sentences.

1. 2 + 4 = __6__
2. 3 + 5 = __8__
3. 4 + 3 = __7__
4. 4 + 1 = __5__
5. 2 + 5 = __7__
6. 4 + 4 = __8__

Page 119

How Many Rabbits?
Look at the pictures and finish the number sentences.

1. 1 + 1 = __2__
2. 3 + 6 = __9__
3. 6 + 1 = __7__
4. 3 + 4 = __7__
5. 4 + 5 = __9__
6. 2 + 3 = __5__

Page 120

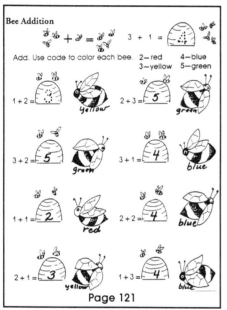

Bee Addition

3 + 1 =

Add. Use code to color each bee.
2—red   4—blue
3—yellow   5—green

1 + 2 = __3__ yellow
2 + 3 = __5__ green
3 + 2 = __5__ green
3 + 1 = __4__ blue
1 + 1 = __2__ red
2 + 2 = __4__ blue
2 + 1 = __3__ yellow
1 + 3 = __4__ blue

Page 121

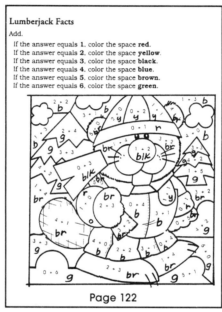

Lumberjack Facts
Add.

If the answer equals **1**, color the space **red**.
If the answer equals **2**, color the space **yellow**.
If the answer equals **3**, color the space **black**.
If the answer equals **4**, color the space **blue**.
If the answer equals **5**, color the space **brown**.
If the answer equals **6**, color the space **green**.

Page 122

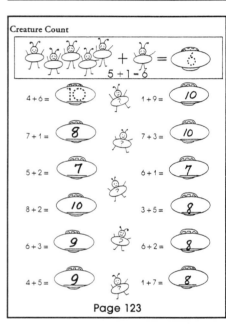

Creature Count

5 + 1 = 6

4 + 6 = __10__
1 + 9 = __10__
7 + 1 = __8__
7 + 3 = __10__
5 + 2 = __7__
6 + 1 = __7__
8 + 2 = __10__
3 + 5 = __8__
6 + 3 = __9__
6 + 2 = __8__
4 + 5 = __9__
1 + 7 = __8__

Page 123

Beary Good
Put counters on each bear to show the addition. Write the sums.

3 + 2 = __5__   5 + 0 = __5__   1 + 6 = __7__   4 + 2 = __6__

$\begin{array}{r}6\\+1\\\hline 7\end{array}$ $\begin{array}{r}3\\+4\\\hline 7\end{array}$ $\begin{array}{r}2\\+3\\\hline 5\end{array}$ $\begin{array}{r}5\\+2\\\hline 7\end{array}$ $\begin{array}{r}7\\+1\\\hline 8\end{array}$ $\begin{array}{r}0\\+2\\\hline 2\end{array}$

$\begin{array}{r}8\\+0\\\hline 8\end{array}$ $\begin{array}{r}4\\+5\\\hline 9\end{array}$ $\begin{array}{r}3\\+6\\\hline 9\end{array}$ $\begin{array}{r}2\\+6\\\hline 8\end{array}$ $\begin{array}{r}3\\+5\\\hline 8\end{array}$ $\begin{array}{r}6\\+2\\\hline 8\end{array}$

Page 124

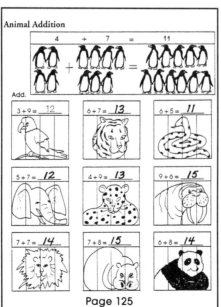

Animal Addition

4 + 7 = 11

Add.

3 + 9 = __12__   6 + 7 = __13__   6 + 5 = __11__
5 + 7 = __12__   4 + 9 = __13__   9 + 6 = __15__
7 + 7 = __14__   7 + 8 = __15__   6 + 8 = __14__

Page 125

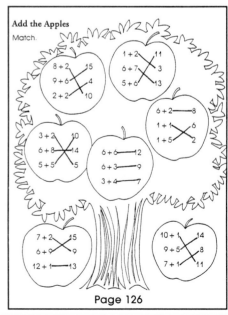

Add the Apples
Match.

8 + 2 — 15
9 + 6 — 4
2 + 2 — 10
1 + 2 — 11
6 + 7 — 3
5 + 6 — 13
6 + 2 — 8
1 + 1 — 6
1 + 5 — 7
3 + 2 — 10
6 + 8 — 14
5 + 5 — 9
6 + 6 — 12
6 + 3 — 9
3 + 4 — 7
7 + 2 — 15
6 + 9 — 9
12 + 1 — 13
10 + 1 — 14
9 + 5 — 8
7 + 1 — 11

Page 126

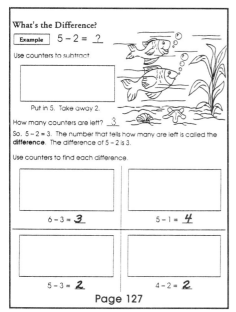

What's the Difference?

Example   5 − 2 = 2

Use counters to subtract

Put in 5. Take away 2.

How many counters are left? 3

So, 5 − 2 = 3. The number that tells how many are left is called the **difference**. The difference of 5 − 2 is 3.

Use counters to find each difference.

6 − 3 = 3   5 − 1 = 4

5 − 3 = 2   4 − 2 = 2

Page 127

Counting Kittens

Use counters. Make a set, then take away. Write how many are left.

Put in 4. Take away 1.   3 are left.

Put in 5. Take away 2.   3 are left.

Put in 6. Take away 1.   5 are left.

Put in 7. Take away 3.   4 are left.

Think of a story for this picture. Write how many are left.   3 are left.

Page 128

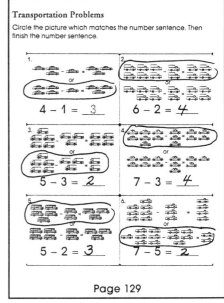

Transportation Problems

Circle the picture which matches the number sentence. Then finish the number sentence.

1. 4 − 1 = 3
2. 6 − 2 = 4
3. 5 − 3 = 2
4. 7 − 3 = 4
5. 5 − 2 = 3
6. 7 − 5 = 2

Page 129

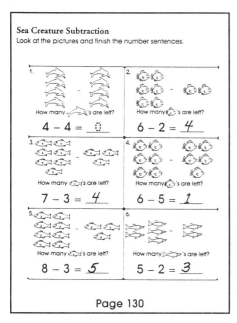

Sea Creature Subtraction

Look at the pictures and finish the number sentences.

1. How many dolphins are left?   4 − 4 = 0
2. How many fish are left?   6 − 2 = 4
3. How many fish are left?   7 − 3 = 4
4. How many fish are left?   6 − 5 = 1
5. How many fish are left?   8 − 3 = 5
6. How many fish are left?   5 − 2 = 3

Page 130

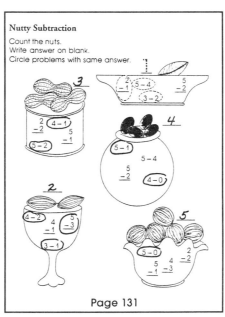

Nutty Subtraction

Count the nuts.
Write answer on blank.
Circle problems with same answer.

3   4   2   5

Page 131

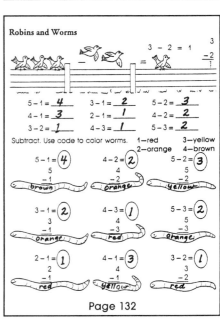

Robins and Worms

3 − 2 = 1

5 − 1 = 4   3 − 1 = 2   5 − 2 = 3
4 − 1 = 3   2 − 1 = 1   4 − 2 = 2
3 − 2 = 1   4 − 3 = 1   5 − 3 = 2

Subtract. Use code to color worms.   1—red   3—yellow
2—orange   4—brown

5 − 1 = 4   4 − 2 = 2   5 − 2 = 3
brown   orange   yellow

3 − 1 = 2   4 − 3 = 1   5 − 3 = 2
orange   red   orange

2 − 1 = 1   4 − 1 = 3   3 − 2 = 1
red   yellow   red

Page 132

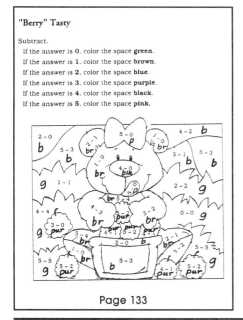

"Berry" Tasty

Subtract.
If the answer is **0**, color the space **green**.
If the answer is **1**, color the space **brown**.
If the answer is **2**, color the space **blue**.
If the answer is **3**, color the space **purple**.
If the answer is **4**, color the space **black**.
If the answer is **5**, color the space **pink**.

Page 133

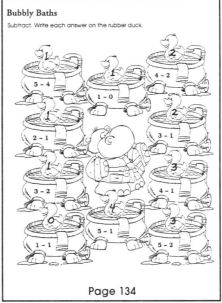

Bubbly Baths

Subtract. Write each answer on the rubber duck.

Page 134

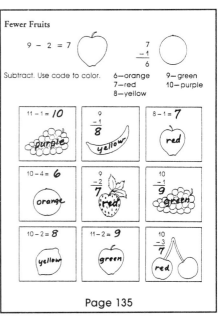

Fewer Fruits

9 − 2 = 7

7 − 1 = 6

Subtract. Use code to color.   6—orange   9—green
7—red   10—purple
8—yellow

11 − 1 = 10   9 − 8 = 1   8 − 1 = 7
purple   yellow   red

10 − 4 = 6   9 − 2 = 7   10 − 1 = 9
orange   red   green

10 − 2 = 8   11 − 2 = 9   10 − 3 = 7
yellow   green   red

Page 135

Sweet Treats

Count the candy.
Write number on blank.
Circle problems with same answer.

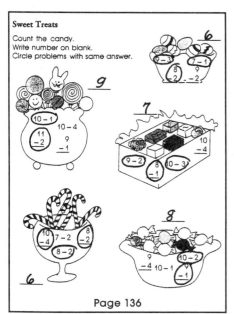

Page 136

A Whale of a Job!

For each problem, put the number of counters needed in the water, then take away by sliding the numbers into the whale's mouth. Then, count how many counters are left in the water to find the difference.

$$\begin{array}{ccccc} 7 & 9 & 6 & 5 & 8 \\ -3 & -2 & -4 & -2 & -3 \\ \hline 4 & 7 & 2 & 3 & 5 \end{array}$$

$$\begin{array}{ccccc} 9 & 6 & 7 & 8 & 5 \\ -3 & -3 & -5 & -2 & -1 \\ \hline 6 & 3 & 2 & 6 & 4 \end{array}$$

$8 - 4 = 4 \qquad 6 - 2 = 4 \qquad 7 - 4 = 3$

Page 137

Hop Along Numbers

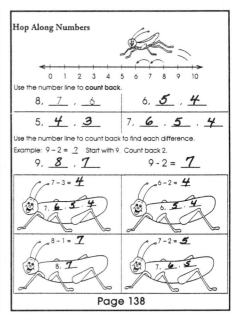

Use the number line to **count back**.

8, 7, 6 | 6, 5, 4

5, 4, 3 | 7, 6, 5, 4

Use the number line to count back to find each difference.

Example: $9 - 2 = 7$ Start with 9. Count back 2.

9, 8, 7 | $9 - 2 = 7$

$7 - 3 = 4$ | $6 - 2 = 4$
7, 6, 5, 4 | 6, 5, 4

$8 - 1 = 7$ | $7 - 2 = 5$
8, 7 | 7, 6, 5

Page 138

Crayon Count

Count crayons. Write number on blank.
Circle problems that name answer.

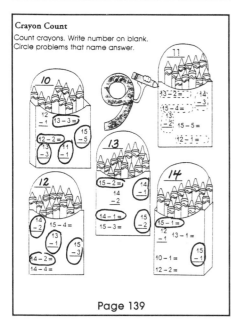

Page 139

Turtle Math—Take It Slow

Color answer:
2—red
3—blue
4—yellow
5—green

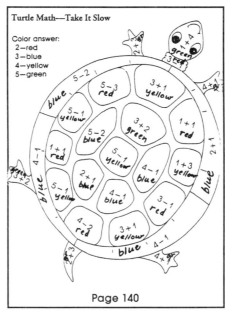

Page 140

It's Show Time

It's time for Packy and Dermit to perform. Look at the problems. Write + or − on each peanut to make the problem correct. Then trace a path from peanut to peanut, connecting each elephant to the correct stool. For Packy, connect all of the + problems. For Dermit, connect all of the − problems.

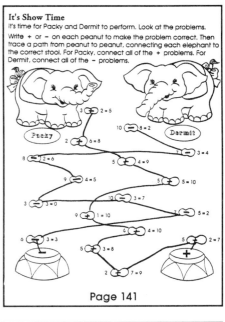

Page 141

Puppy Problems

Look at the pictures and finish the number sentences.

1. $5 \oplus 6 = 11$
2. $11 \ominus 4 = 7$
3. $12 \ominus 7 = 5$
4. $7 \oplus 6 = 13$
5. $5 \oplus 5 = 10$
6. $8 \oplus 6 = 14$

Page 142

Calling All Cats

Look at the pictures and finish the number sentences.

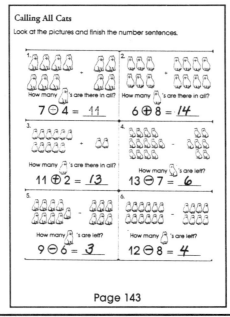

1. How many 's are there in all?
$7 \ominus 4 = 11$
2. How many 's are there in all?
$6 \oplus 8 = 14$
3. How many 's are there in all?
$11 \oplus 2 = 13$
4. How many 's are left?
$13 \ominus 7 = 6$
5. How many 's are left?
$9 \ominus 6 = 3$
6. How many 's are left?
$12 \ominus 8 = 4$

Page 143

What Was the Question?

Draw a line under the question that matches the picture. Then finish the number sentence.

1. How many 's are there in all?
How many 's are left?
$11 - 7 = 4$
2. How many 's are there in all?
How many 's are left?
$4 + 5 = 9$
3. How many 's are there in all?
How many 's are left?
$8 - 3 = 5$
4. How many 's are there in all?
How many 's are left?
$10 - 4 = 6$
5. How many 's are there in all?
How many 's are left?
$5 + 6 = 11$
6. How many 's are there in all?
How many 's are left?
$8 + 4 = 12$

Page 144

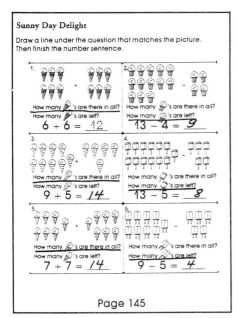

Sunny Day Delight

Draw a line under the question that matches the picture.
Then finish the number sentence.

1. How many 🍦's are there in all?
How many 🍦's are left?
$6 + 6 =$ 12

2. How many 😊's are there in all?
How many 😊's are left?
$13 - 4 =$ 9

3. How many 🍦's are there in all?
How many 🍦's are left?
$9 + 5 =$ 14

4. How many 🍦's are there in all?
How many 🍦's are left?
$13 - 5 =$ 8

5. How many 🍦's are there in all?
How many 🍦's are left?
$7 + 7 =$ 14

6. How many 🍦's are there in all?
How many 🍦's are left?
$9 - 5 =$ 4

Page 145

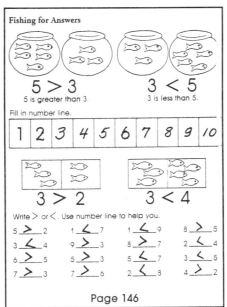

Fishing for Answers

$5 > 3$
5 is greater than 3.

$3 < 5$
3 is less than 5.

Fill in number line.

| 1 | 2 | 3 | 4 | 5 | 6 | 7 | 8 | 9 | 10 |

$3 > 2$ $3 < 4$

Write > or <. Use number line to help you.

$5 > 2$ $1 < 7$ $1 < 9$ $8 > 5$
$3 < 4$ $9 > 3$ $8 > 7$ $2 < 4$
$6 > 5$ $5 > 3$ $5 < 7$ $3 < 5$
$7 > 3$ $7 > 6$ $2 < 8$ $4 > 2$

Page 146

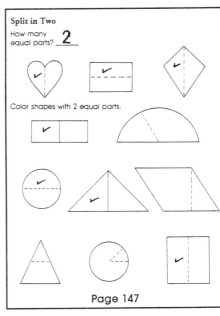

Split in Two

How many equal parts? 2

Color shapes with 2 equal parts.

Page 147

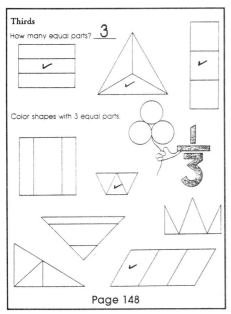

Thirds

How many equal parts? 3

Color shapes with 3 equal parts.

Page 148

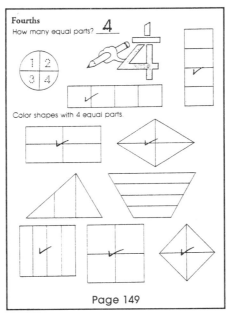

Fourths

How many equal parts? 4

Color shapes with 4 equal parts.

Page 149

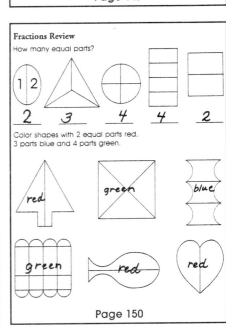

Fractions Review

How many equal parts?

$\frac{1\ 2}{2}$ $\frac{}{3}$ $\frac{}{4}$ $\frac{}{4}$ $\frac{}{2}$

Color shapes with 2 equal parts red,
3 parts blue and 4 parts green.

red   green   blue

green   red   red

Page 150

A Race!

first   second   third   fourth   fifth   sixth   seventh

Write the correct word to tell where each runner placed in the race.

1. sixth
2. fifth
3. seventh
4. fourth
5. first
6. third
7. second

Flip Fun! Draw a prize you would like to receive for winning a race.

Page 151

Flags First

Color the ninth flag red.
Write O on the second flag.
Color the eighth flag blue.
Write D on the fourth flag.
Color the sixth flag yellow.
Write G on the first flag.
Color the tenth flag purple.
Write O on the third flag.
Color the seventh flag green.
Color the fifth flag orange.

Page 152

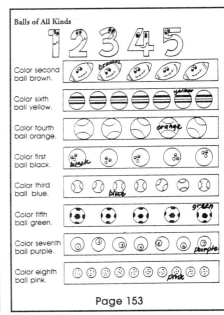

Balls of All Kinds

Color second ball brown.
Color sixth ball yellow.
Color fourth ball orange.
Color first ball black.
Color third ball blue.
Color fifth ball green.
Color seventh ball purple.
Color eighth ball pink.

Page 153

Henny Penny

How much money?

Example

1¢ 1 penny 1 cent

1¢ 1¢ 1¢
1¢ 1¢ = 5 ¢

1¢ 1¢ 1¢ 1¢
1¢ 1¢ = 6 ¢

1¢ 1¢ = 2 ¢

1¢ 1¢ 1¢ = 3 ¢

1¢ 1¢ 1¢
1¢ = 4 ¢

1¢ 1¢ 1¢ 1¢
1¢ 1¢ 1¢ 1¢ = 8 ¢

1¢ 1¢ 1¢ 1¢ 1¢ 1¢ 1¢ = 7 ¢

Page 154

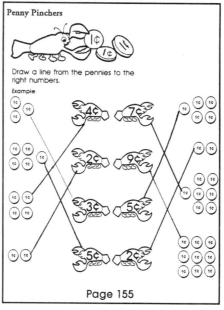

Penny Pinchers

Draw a line from the pennies to the right numbers.

Example

Page 155

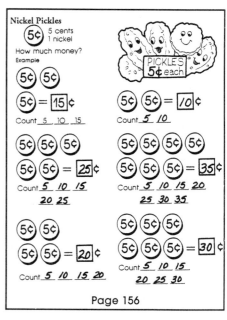

Nickel Pickles

5¢ 5 cents 1 nickel

How much money?

Example

PICKLES 5¢ each

5¢ 5¢
5¢ = 15 ¢
Count 5 10 15

5¢ 5¢ = 10 ¢
Count 5 10

5¢ 5¢ 5¢
5¢ 5¢ = 25 ¢
Count 5 10 15
20 25

5¢ 5¢ 5¢ 5¢
5¢ 5¢ 5¢ = 35 ¢
Count 5 10 15 20
25 30 35

5¢ 5¢
5¢ 5¢ = 20 ¢
Count 5 10 15 20

5¢ 5¢ 5¢
5¢ 5¢ 5¢ = 30 ¢
Count 5 10 15
20 25 30

Page 156

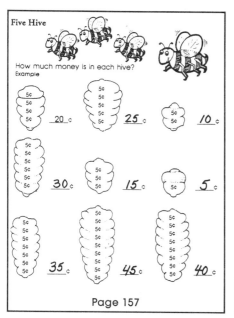

Five Hive

How much money is in each hive?

Example

20 ¢   25 ¢   10 ¢

30 ¢   15 ¢   5 ¢

35 ¢   45 ¢   40 ¢

Page 157

Money Bunnies

Count the coins. Write the amount under each bunny's carrot.

Example

7¢   11¢

17¢   21¢

12¢   14¢

Page 158

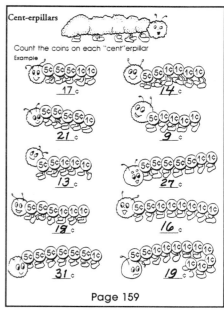

Cent-erpillars

Count the coins on each "cent"erpillar

Example

17 ¢   14 ¢

21 ¢   9 ¢

13 ¢   27 ¢

18 ¢   16 ¢

31 ¢   19 ¢

Page 159

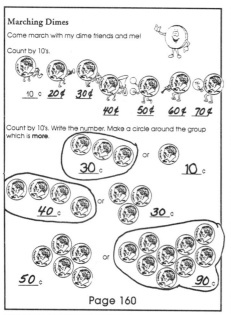

Marching Dimes

Come march with my dime friends and me!

Count by 10's.

10 ¢ 20¢ 30¢ 40¢ 50¢ 60¢ 70¢

Count by 10's. Write the number. Make a circle around the group which is **more**.

30 ¢   or   10 ¢

40 ¢   or   30 ¢

50 ¢   or   90 ¢

Page 160

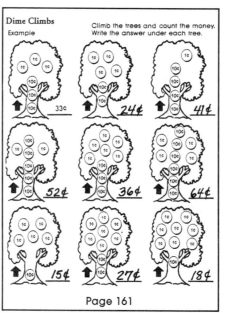

Dime Climbs

Example

Climb the trees and count the money. Write the answer under each tree.

33¢   24¢   41¢

52¢   36¢   64¢

15¢   27¢   18¢

Page 161

Buy and Buy

Circle the coins to equal the right amount.

Example

32¢   26¢

21¢   14¢

54¢   31¢

44¢   42¢

Page 162

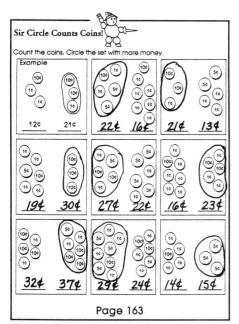

Sir Circle Counts Coins!

Count the coins. Circle the set with more money.

Page 163

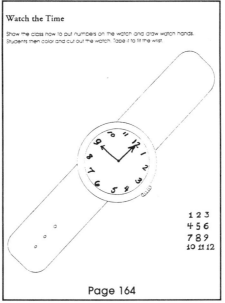

Watch the Time

Show the class how to put numbers on the watch and draw watch hands. Students then color and cut out the watch. Tape it to fit the wrist.

Page 164

Hickory Dickory Dock

What time is it?

Page 165

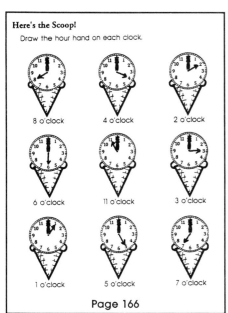

Here's the Scoop!

Draw the hour hand on each clock.

Page 166

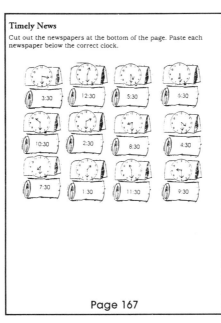

Timely News

Cut out the newspapers at the bottom of the page. Paste each newspaper below the correct clock.

Page 167

Who "Nose" These Times?

Write the time under each clock. Color the noses.

Page 168

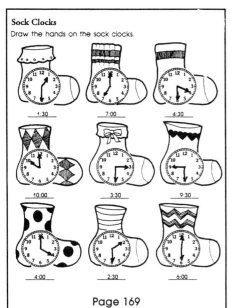

Sock Clocks

Draw the hands on the sock clocks.

Page 169

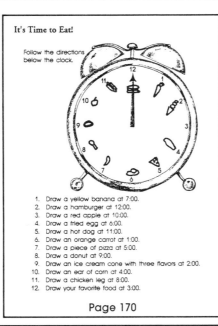

It's Time to Eat!

Follow the directions below the clock.

1. Draw a yellow banana at 7:00.
2. Draw a hamburger at 12:00.
3. Draw a red apple at 10:00.
4. Draw a fried egg at 6:00.
5. Draw a hot dog at 11:00.
6. Draw an orange carrot at 1:00.
7. Draw a piece of pizza at 5:00.
8. Draw a donut at 9:00.
9. Draw an ice cream cone with three flavors at 2:00.
10. Draw an ear of corn at 4:00.
11. Draw a chicken leg at 8:00.
12. Draw your favorite food at 3:00.

Page 170

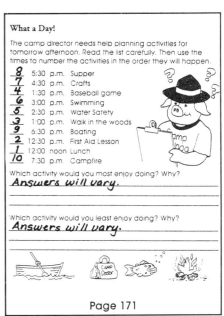

What a Day!

The camp director needs help planning activities for tomorrow afternoon. Read the list carefully. Then use the times to number the activities in the order they will happen.

8 — 5:30 p.m. Supper
7 — 4:30 p.m. Crafts
4 — 1:30 p.m. Baseball game
6 — 3:00 p.m. Swimming
5 — 2:30 p.m. Water Safety
3 — 1:00 p.m. Walk in the woods
9 — 6:30 p.m. Boating
2 — 12:30 p.m. First Aid Lesson
1 — 12:00 noon Lunch
10 — 7:30 p.m. Campfire

Which activity would you most enjoy doing? Why?
Answers will vary.

Which activity would you least enjoy doing? Why?
Answers will vary.

Page 171

It's About Time

There are many ways we measure time. A year is made of 365 days. A week has seven days. A day has 24 hours. An hour is made of 60 minutes. A minute is made of 60 seconds. A second goes very quickly. Can you blink your eyes in one second?

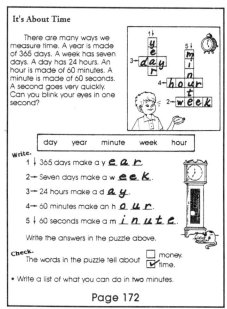

Write. day year minute week hour

1 ↓ 365 days make a y **e a r**

2 → Seven days make a w **e e k**.

3 → 24 hours make a d **a y**.

4 → 60 minutes make an h **o u r**.

5 ↓ 60 seconds make a m **i n u t e**.

Write the answers in the puzzle above.

Check.
The words in the puzzle tell about ☐ money. ☑ time.

• Write a list of what you can do in two minutes.

Page 172

Fun Days

There are seven days in a week. Saturday and Sunday are the weekend days. You go to school the other five days. Which day do you like best?

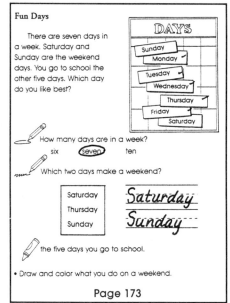

How many days are in a week?
six (seven) ten

Which two days make a weekend?

Saturday	*Saturday*
Thursday	*Sunday*
Sunday	

the five days you go to school.

• Draw and color what you do on a weekend.

Page 173

Hmm, What Month Is It?

There are twelve months in a year. The first month is January. The last month is December. Some months have 31 days. Some months have 30 days. February is the shortest month with 28 days. Can you name the months of the year?

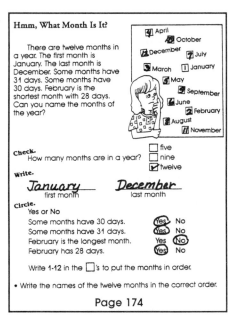

Check.
How many months are in a year? ☐ five ☐ nine ☑ twelve

Write.
January first month   *December* last month

Circle.
Yes or No
Some months have 30 days. (Yes) No
Some months have 31 days. (Yes) No
February is the longest month. Yes (No)
February has 28 days. (Yes) No

Write 1-12 in the ☐'s to put the months in order.

• Write the names of the twelve months in the correct order.

Page 174

How Did You Do That?

You use many parts of your body to do even the simplest activities.

Read each activity and write the body parts you would use to do that activity.

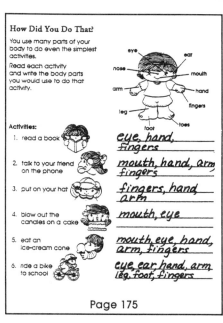

Activities:

1. read a book — *eye, hand, fingers*

2. talk to your friend on the phone — *mouth, hand, arm, fingers*

3. put on your hat — *fingers, hand, arm*

4. blow out the candles on a cake — *mouth, eye*

5. eat an ice-cream cone — *mouth, eye, hand, arm, fingers*

6. ride a bike to school — *eye, ear, hand, arm, leg, foot, fingers*

Page 175

Body Buddies

Follow the numbers to print a word that is part of your body. Then color each part.

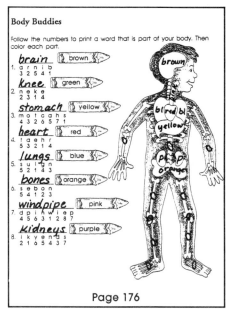

brain 〈brown〉
1. a r n i b
   3 2 5 4 1

knee 〈green〉
2. n e k e
   2 3 1 4

stomach 〈yellow〉
3. m o t c a h s
   4 3 2 6 5 7 1

heart 〈red〉
4. t a e h r
   5 3 2 1 4

lungs 〈blue〉
5. s u l g n
   5 2 1 4 3

bones 〈orange〉
6. s e b o n
   5 4 1 2 3

windpipe 〈pink〉
7. d p i h w i e p
   4 5 6 1 3 2 8 7

kidneys 〈purple〉
8. i k y e n d s
   2 1 6 5 4 3 7

Page 176

It Makes Sense to Me

Our five senses help us understand and make "sense" of our world. Look at each group of pictures. Decide which sense (see, hear, smell, taste, or feel) is used for most items in each group of pictures. Write the sense on the line below each group. Then put an X on the one picture that does not belong in each group.

hear   *feel*

taste

smell   *see*

Page 177

Outfitted for Health

Read the phrases in the Word Bank. Write only the **good** health habits on the lines.

Word Bank			
Take a bath.	Eat a lot of sweets	Stay up all night.
Drink water.	Get plenty of sleep.	Keep cuts clean.
Sit all day.	Never wash your hands.	Brush your teeth.
Exercise.	Eat healthy foods.	

1. *Take a bath.*
2. *Drink water.*
3. *Exercise.*
4. *Get plenty of sleep.*
5. *Eat healthy foods.*
6. *Keep cuts clean.*
7. *Brush your teeth.*

Page 178

Exercise!

Do you like to exercise? Exercise is good for you. Walking and running are good ways to exercise. So are swimming and biking. Some people like to do push-ups, sit-ups and jumping jacks. Exercise can help you feel good. It can make your body stronger, too. What is your favorite kind of exercise?

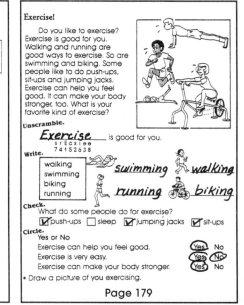

Unscramble.
Exercise is good for you.
s r E c x i e e
7 4 1 5 2 6 3 8

Write.
| walking |
| swimming |
| biking |
| running |

swimming *walking*
running *biking*

Check.
What do some people do for exercise?
☑ push-ups ☐ sleep ☑ jumping jacks ☑ sit-ups

Circle.
Yes or No
Exercise can help you feel good. (Yes) No
Exercise is very easy. Yes (No)
Exercise can make your body stronger. (Yes) No

• Draw a picture of you exercising.

Page 179

Pyramiding Foods

Read the names of the foods in the Word Bank. Write the words on the lines under the correct food group.

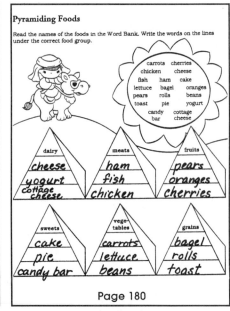

Word Bank: carrots, cherries, chicken, cheese, fish, ham, cake, lettuce, bagel, oranges, pears, rolls, beans, toast, pie, yogurt, candy bar, cottage cheese

dairy
cheese
yogurt
cottage cheese

meats
ham
fish
chicken

fruits
pears
oranges
cherries

sweets
cake
pie
candy bar

vegetables
carrots
lettuce
beans

grains
bagel
rolls
toast

Page 180

Leaf Shapes

All leaves are not the same. They have different shapes. There are four common shapes.

Draw a line to match the leaf with its shape.

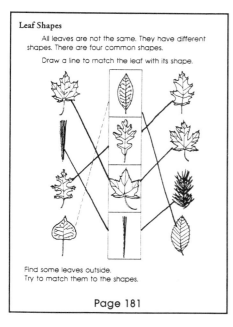

Find some leaves outside.
Try to match them to the shapes.

Page 181

Tree Parts

Trees have three main parts. They are the trunk, the roots, and the leaves. Each part has a special job. Each part helps the tree.
Cut out the name of each part.
Cut out the job of each part.
Paste them on the picture.
Color the tree.

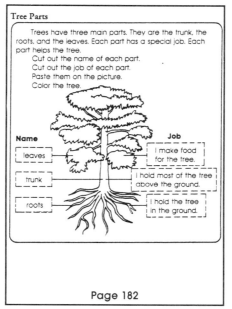

Name

| leaves |
| trunk |
| roots |

Job

I make food for the tree.

I hold most of the tree above the ground.

I hold the tree in the ground.

Page 182

Leaf Study

Put a leaf under the box on this paper. Rub the paper with the side of your crayon. Use the ruler at the bottom to measure your leaf.

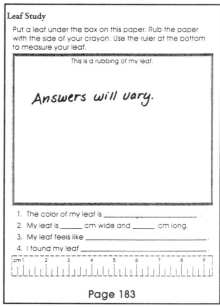

This is a rubbing of my leaf.

Answers will vary.

1. The color of my leaf is _____
2. My leaf is _____ cm wide and _____ cm long.
3. My leaf feels like _____
4. I found my leaf _____

Page 183

Food Factories

Green leaves are like little factories. They make food for the tree. Leaves need sunshine, air, and water to make food.

Leaves change in the fall. They lose their green color. Then they cannot make food for the tree.

Draw a leaf.
This leaf can make food.
Color it green.
Write the correct word.

Draw another leaf.
This leaf cannot make food.
Color it with pretty fall colors.

green   yellow

Food is made by *green* leaves.

shade   sunshine

Leaves need *sunshine* to make food.

can   cannot

Leaves *cannot* make food in the fall.

Page 184

My Leaf Collection

Attach a leaf and fill in the blanks.
Teacher: Provide each student with three or more copies of this page so booklets can be made.

Answers will vary.

Tree _____
Location _____
Date _____

Page 185

From Acorn to Mighty Oak

Some trees drop their seeds in the spring. Other trees drop their seeds in the fall. The seeds grow up. Do you know what they grow up to be?

Show how the acorn grows into a mighty oak tree. Write first, second, or third under the pictures to put them in order. Color the pictures.

first   *third*   *second*

Finish the story.
I am a little acorn. One day _____

Stories will vary.

Page 186

Plant Parts

A plant has many parts. Each part has a special job.

Word Bank roots   stem
flower   leaf

Label the parts of the plant.

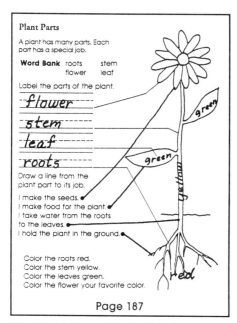

flower
stem
leaf
roots

Draw a line from the plant part to its job.
I make the seeds.
I make food for the plant.
I take water from the roots to the leaves.
I hold the plant in the ground.

Color the roots red.
Color the stem yellow.
Color the leaves green.
Color the flower your favorite color.

Page 187

Growing Words

Write each word on the line below the correct picture.

pumpkin   seed   sprout   flower   plant

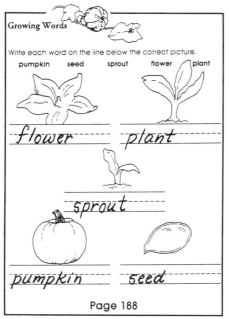

flower   *plant*

sprout

pumpkin   *seed*

Page 188

Edible Plant Parts

We eat many plant parts. Sometimes we eat just the fruit. Sometimes we eat just the leaves. We also might eat the stem, the root, or the seed.

Draw a line from the picture to the name of the plant part.
Color the plant part.

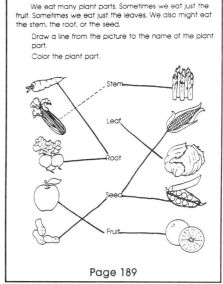

Stem
Leaf
Root
Seed
Fruit

Page 189

Plant It Right!

Mr. Right and Mr. Wrong planted gardens. Mr. Right planted his garden in the sun. Mr. Wrong planted his garden in the shade. Both of them gave their gardens love and care.

Draw what Mr. Right's garden will look like.

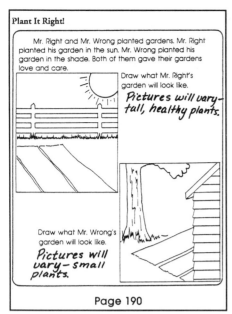

Pictures will vary— tall, healthy plants.

Draw what Mr. Wrong's garden will look like.

Pictures will vary—small plants.

Page 190

Water, Please!

Mrs. Right planted her flower seeds last week. She planted them in the sun. She gave her flowers water.

Mrs. Wrong planted her flower seeds last week. She planted them in the sun. But she forgot to give them water.

Draw what Mrs. Right's flowers will look like.

Draw what Mrs. Wrong's flowers will look like.

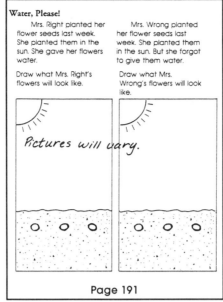

Pictures will vary.

Page 191

All in the Family

Put an X on the animal that does not belong.

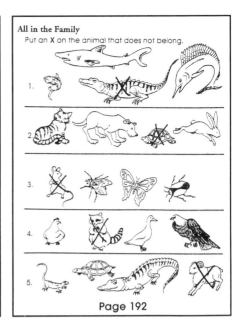

1.
2.
3.
4.
5.

Page 192

Animals on the Go

How do these animals move?
Write **walk**, **fly** or **swim**.

swim   walk   fly

swim   walk   fly

fly   walk   swim

Page 193

Pond Community

Many animals make their homes in a pond community, but some of the animals in this picture do not belong.

Draw an X on the animals that do **not** belong.

Page 194

Grassland Community

Many animals make their homes in a grassland community, but some of the animals in this picture do not belong.

Draw an X on the animals that do **not** belong.

Page 195

Ocean Community

Many animals make their homes in an ocean community, but some of the animals in this picture do not belong.

Draw an X on the animals that do **not** belong.

Page 196

Forest Community

Many animals make their homes in a forest community, but some of the animals in this picture do not belong.

Draw an X on the animals that do **not** belong.

Page 197

Animals at Home

Did you ever see a fish living in a tree? Of course you didn't! Fish live in the water. Help the animals find their homes.

Cut out each animal.
Paste it on its home.
Color the picture.

bee

robin

squirrel

fish

Page 198

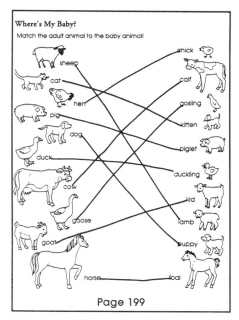

Where's My Baby?

Match the adult animal to the baby animal!

- sheep — lamb
- cat — kitten
- hen — chick
- pig — piglet
- dog — puppy
- duck — duckling
- cow — calf
- goose — gosling
- goat — kid
- horse — foal

Page 199

Feathered Friends

Name the parts of the bird.

feathers *bill* *wings* *feet*

Read the riddle. Name each bird part.

I keep a bird warm and dry. What am I? *feathers*
I help a bird stand or swim. What am I? *feet*
I help a bird eat. What am I? *bill*
I make a bird fly high in the sky. What am I? *wings*

Word Bank			
feathers	feet	bill	wings

Page 200

My Bird List

Bird watchers keep a list of all the different kinds of birds they have seen. They also keep track of the date and location. Begin a list of your own using the chart below.

Bird	Date	Location
Lists will vary.		

Page 201

I Slither and Crawl

Do the puzzle about reptiles.
Color only the reptiles.

Across
2. A reptile's skin has *scales*
5. A *snake* is a reptile with no legs.

Down
1. A *turtle* is a reptile with a hard shell on its back.
3. Reptiles are *cold* -blooded animals.
4. Baby reptiles hatch from *eggs*

Word Bank				
eggs	cold	scales	snake	turtle

Page 202

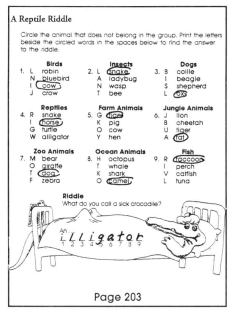

A Reptile Riddle

Circle the animal that does not belong in the group. Print the letters beside the circled words in the spaces below to find the answer to the riddle.

Birds
1. L robin
 N bluebird
 I cow
 J crow

Insects
2. L snake
 A ladybug
 N wasp
 T bee

Dogs
3. B collie
 I beagle
 S shepherd
 L ox

Reptiles
4. R snake
 I horse
 G turtle
 W alligator

Farm Animals
5. G tiger
 K pig
 O cow
 Y hen

Jungle Animals
6. L lion
 B cheetah
 U tiger
 A rat

Zoo Animals
7. M bear
 O giraffe
 T dog
 F zebra

Ocean Animals
8. H octopus
 T whale
 K shark
 O camel

Fish
9. R raccoon
 I perch
 V catfish
 L tuna

Riddle
What do you call a sick crocodile?

An *ILLIgator*
1 2 3 4 5 6 7 8 9

Page 203

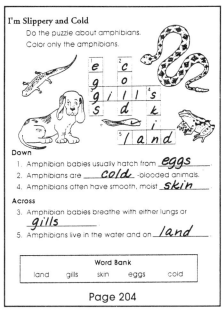

I'm Slippery and Cold

Do the puzzle about amphibians.
Color only the amphibians.

Down
1. Amphibian babies usually hatch from *eggs*
2. Amphibians are *cold* -blooded animals.
4. Amphibians often have smooth, moist *skin*

Across
3. Amphibian babies breathe with either lungs or *gills*
5. Amphibians live in the water and on *land*

Word Bank				
land	gills	skin	eggs	cold

Page 204

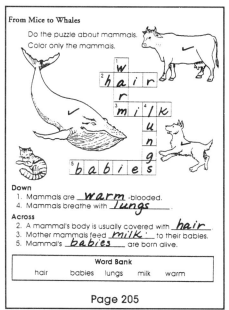

From Mice to Whales

Do the puzzle about mammals.
Color only the mammals.

Down
1. Mammals are *warm* -blooded.
4. Mammals breathe with *lungs*

Across
2. A mammal's body is usually covered with *hair*
3. Mother mammals feed *milk* to their babies.
5. Mammal's *babies* are born alive.

Word Bank				
hair	babies	lungs	milk	warm

Page 205

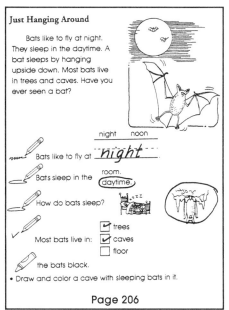

Just Hanging Around

Bats like to fly at night. They sleep in the daytime. A bat sleeps by hanging upside down. Most bats live in trees and caves. Have you ever seen a bat?

night   noon

Bats like to fly at *night*

Bats sleep in the daytime room.

How do bats sleep?

Most bats live in:
- ☑ trees
- ☑ caves
- ☐ floor

_____ the bats black.

• Draw and color a cave with sleeping bats in it.

Page 206

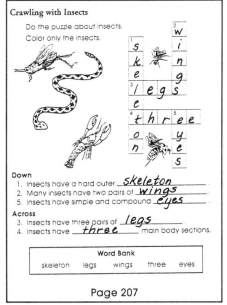

Crawling with Insects

Do the puzzle about insects.
Color only the insects.

Down
1. Insects have a hard outer *skeleton*
2. Many insects have two pairs of *wings*
5. Insects have simple and compound *eyes*

Across
3. Insects have three pairs of *legs*
4. Insects have *three* main body sections.

Word Bank				
skeleton	legs	wings	three	eyes

Page 207

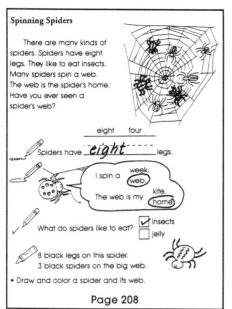

Spinning Spiders

There are many kinds of spiders. Spiders have eight legs. They like to eat insects. Many spiders spin a web. The web is the spider's home. Have you ever seen a spider's web?

eight   four

Spiders have _eight_ legs.

I spin a week.
~~web.~~ **web**

The web is my kite.
~~home.~~ **home**

What do spiders like to eat? ☑ insects
☐ jelly

8 black legs on this spider.
3 black spiders on the big web.

• Draw and color a spider and its web.

Page 208

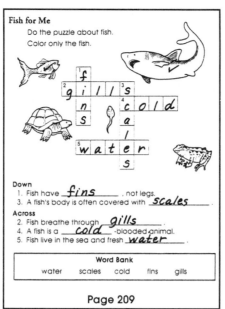

Fish for Me

Do the puzzle about fish.
Color only the fish.

f
g i l l s
i   c o l d
n   a
s   l
water   s

Down
1. Fish have _fins_ , not legs.
3. A fish's body is often covered with _scales_

Across
2. Fish breathe through _gills_
4. A fish is a _cold_ -blooded animal.
5. Fish live in the sea and fresh _water_

Word Bank
water   scales   cold   fins   gills

Page 209

"Hatch" Something Up

Many animals are hatched from eggs.
Read the clues. Then use the Word Bank to write the name of the correct animal on each egg.

alligator
I am a reptile.
I have big, sharp teeth.
I live near a river.

mud turtle
I live most of my life in water.
I eat tadpoles and water insects.
I can pull myself inside my shell.

duck
I have feathers.
I have webbed feet.
I swim in a pond.
I quack with my bill.

chick
I have feathers.
I live on a farm.
I have wings and make peeping sounds with my beak.

frog
I live near water.
I eat insects.
I have a tail when I hatch, but I lose it as I grow.
I can leap up to six feet.

Word Bank
snake   frog   chick   mud turtle   duck   alligator

Page 210

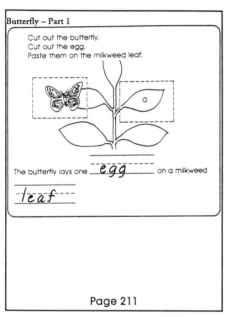

Butterfly – Part 1

Cut out the butterfly.
Cut out the egg.
Paste them on the milkweed leaf.

The butterfly lays one _egg_ on a milkweed _leaf_

Page 211

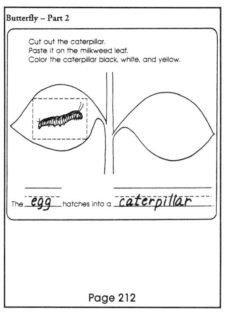

Butterfly – Part 2

Cut out the caterpillar.
Paste it on the milkweed leaf.
Color the caterpillar black, white, and yellow.

The _egg_ hatches into a _caterpillar_

Page 212

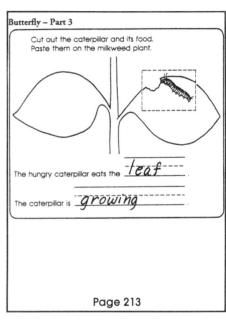

Butterfly – Part 3

Cut out the caterpillar and its food.
Paste them on the milkweed plant.

The hungry caterpillar eats the _leaf_

The caterpillar is _growing_

Page 213

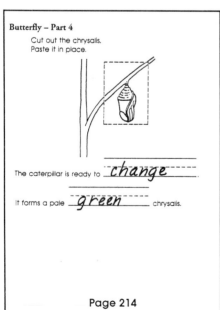

Butterfly – Part 4

Cut out the chrysalis.
Paste it in place.

The caterpillar is ready to _change_

It forms a pale _green_ chrysalis.

Page 214

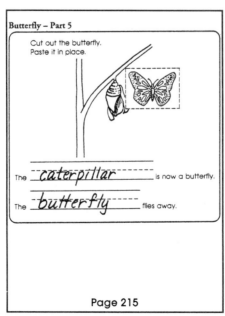

Butterfly – Part 5

Cut out the butterfly.
Paste it in place.

The _caterpillar_ is now a butterfly.

The _butterfly_ flies away.

Page 215

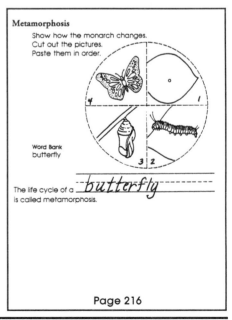

Metamorphosis

Show how the monarch changes.
Cut out the pictures.
Paste them in order.

Word Bank
butterfly

The life cycle of a _butterfly_ is called metamorphosis.

Page 216

Migration

Cut out the animals.
Paste them in place.

It is hard to find ___food___ in the winter.

It is hard to stay ___warm___ in the winter.

Some animals move to warmer places then.
This is called migration.

Page 217

Active Animals

Cut out the animals.
Paste them in place.

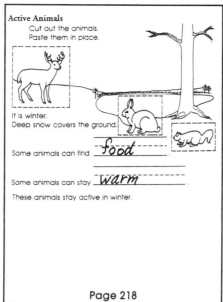

It is winter.
Deep snow covers the ground.

Some animals can find ___food___

Some animals can stay ___warm___

These animals stay active in winter.

Page 218

Storing Food

Cut out the beaver.
Paste him by the hole in the ice.
Trace the path to the beaver's lodge.

Some animals store food for ___winter___

The beaver stores food in his ___lodge___

Page 219

Hibernation

Cut out the fat woodchuck.
Paste him by his hole.
Trace the path to the woodchuck's home.

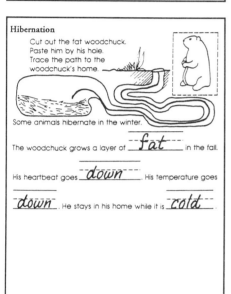

Some animals hibernate in the winter.

The woodchuck grows a layer of ___fat___ in the fall.

His heartbeat goes ___down___ . His temperature goes

___down___ . He stays in his home while it is ___cold___

Page 220

Animals in Winter

Cut out the animal.
Paste it in its place.
Write the animal's name.

This animal hibernates in the winter.

___woodchuck___

This animal migrates in the winter.

___bird___

This animal stays active in the winter.

___rabbit___

This animal stores food for the winter.

___beaver___

Page 221

Animal Homes

Follow the directions below to finish the picture.

1. Draw a fish in the lake.
2. Draw a whale in the ocean.
3. Draw a dog beside the river.
4. Draw a goat on the mountain.
5. Draw a bird on the island.
6. Now color the picture.

Page 222

Blooms and Birds

It is warm in the spring. Flowers begin to bloom. Trees have new leaves. Birds make their nests and lay eggs. Do you like to fly a kite in the spring?

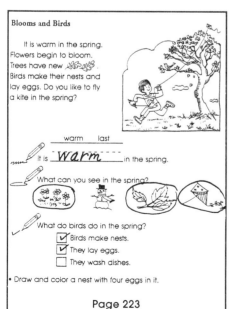

    warm   last

It is ___warm___ in the spring.

What can you see in the spring?

What do birds do in the spring?
- ☑ Birds make nests.
- ☑ They lay eggs.
- ☐ They wash dishes.

• Draw and color a nest with four eggs in it.

Page 223

Fun in the Sun

Summer can be very hot. It is the time when kids are out of school. They have fun playing with friends, swimming to keep cool, and sometimes going on family picnics and vacations.

    purple   hot

Summer can be very ___hot___

What happens in the summer?
- ☑ Kids are out of school.
- ☐ Skunks go on picnics.
- ☑ Kids play with friends.

What do you like to do in the summer?

___Answers will vary.___

• Draw and color a picture of your family on vacation.

Page 224

Autumn Leaves

The air gets cool in the autumn. Kids go back to school. Animals store food for the winter. Leaves turn red, yellow and orange. It is a pretty time of the year.

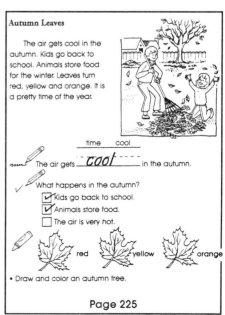

    time   cool

The air gets ___cool___ in the autumn.

What happens in the autumn?
- ☑ Kids go back to school.
- ☑ Animals store food.
- ☐ The air is very hot.

red   yellow   orange

• Draw and color an autumn tree.

Page 225

Winter Warm-ups

Winter can be cold and snowy. Animals stay near each other to keep warm. People wear coats, hats and . Kids can make a snowman. It is fun to play in the snow.

Winter can be: ☑ cold ☑ snowy ☐ purple

like   warm

We try to stay __warm__

What do people wear in the winter?
gloves   hat   pan   coat

a black ▨ on the ☃.

• Draw and color a snowman.

Page 226

The Four Seasons

1. Cut out and paste the season words on the correct boxes below.

2. Color the clothes for:
   Fall – blue; Winter – red;
   Spring – green; Summer – yellow

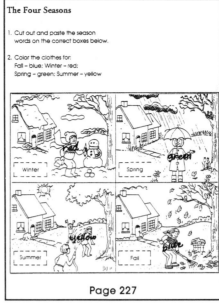

Winter (red)   Spring (green)
Summer (yellow)   Fall (blue)

Page 227

Frederick's Furry Friends

Draw picture details of the four seasons around each of Frederick's furry friends. 🖍 the pictures and each mouse.

Pictures will vary.

Spring Mouse   Summer Mouse

Fall Mouse   Winter Mouse

Page 228

Magnetic Attraction

Draw a line from the magnet to each thing that it can pull.

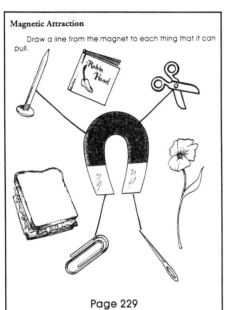

Page 229

Sticky Hunt

What things will a magnet stick to?
Make lists of the things in your room that will and will not stick to a magnet. *Answers will vary.*

Magnets stick to:	Magnets do not stick to:

Caution: Do not try your magnet on these things.
TV   Computer disks
VCR   Cassette tapes
Computer   Video tapes
Radio   Credit cards
Tape recorder   Telephone

Page 230

Opposites Attract

Every magnet has a north pole and a south pole. When you hold two magnets together, this is what happens:

If a north pole and a south pole are next to each other, the magnets attract each other.

S → N   S ← N

If two north poles or two south poles are next to each other, the magnets repel each other.

S ← N   S → N

Tell what each pair of magnets below will do. If the magnets will attract each other, color them red. If the magnets will repel each other, color them blue.

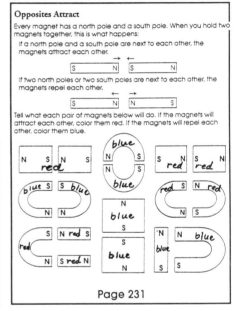

Page 231

Our Planet Earth

Earth is a planet. It is the planet where we live. Earth has land and water. It gets light and heat from the sun. Earth has one moon. Many people think there is life on other planets. Earth is the only planet that we know has life. Do you think there is life on other planets?

Unscramble.
Earth is the __planet__ where we live.
l e t p n a
2 5 6 1 4 3

Check.
☑ I have land and water.
☑ I get light and heat from the sun.
☐ I have five moons.
☑ I have one moon.
☑ I am a planet.

Circle.
Earth is the only planet that we know has (stars. / (life.))

Color.
Draw one yellow moon in the picture.

• Draw and color a picture of Earth.

Page 232

Man on the Moon

Do you ever look at the moon at night? The moon travels around the Earth. It gets its light from the sun. Men have gone to the moon in spaceships. They have walked on the moon. They even came back with moon rocks to study. Would you like to walk on the moon?

Circle.
The moon travels around the (room. / (Earth.))

Write.
The moon gets its light from the __sun__
Earth   sun

Check.
How did men go to the moon? ☑ spaceships ☐ automobiles

Circle.
Yes or No
Men have walked on the moon. ((Yes) / No)

Circle.
What did men bring back from the moon? (stars / (rocks))

Color.
Draw a red spaceship on the moon.

• Draw what you would do if you went to the moon.

Page 233

A Falling Star

Have you ever seen a falling star? Falling stars are not really stars. They are small pieces of rock. As falling stars fall, they get hot and burn. They look big because they give off so much light. That is why they are so bright in the night sky. Did you know that meteor is another name for a falling star?

Circle.
Yes or No
A falling star is really a star.   Yes (No)
Falling stars are pieces of rock.   (Yes) No
Falling stars burn as they fall.   (Yes) No

Check.
Why does a falling star give off light?
☑ It gets hot and burns.
☐ It has a light bulb in it.

Unscramble.
Another name for a falling star is __meteor__
e r m o t e
2 6 1 5 3 4

Color.
Draw two yellow falling stars in the picture.

• Write a poem about a falling star.

Page 234

Far Out!

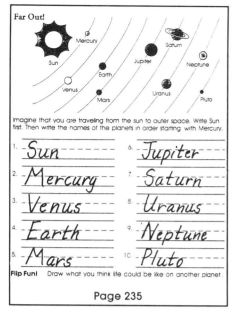

Imagine that you are traveling from the sun to outer space. Write Sun first. Then write the names of the planets in order starting with Mercury.

1. Sun
2. Mercury
3. Venus
4. Earth
5. Mars
6. Jupiter
7. Saturn
8. Uranus
9. Neptune
10. Pluto

Flip Fun! Draw what you think life could be like on another planet.

Page 235

Twinkling Starlights

Stars change as they get older. They start out big and then shrink. As they shrink, they change color. Color the stars the correct color.

red   orange   yellow   blue

Look at all of these stars. Color each star the correct color. Then draw a circle around the youngest stars and a box around the oldest ones.

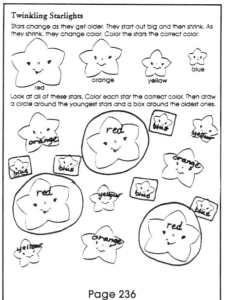

Page 236

Me, Myself, and I

1. Tell about yourself on the lines below.
2. Then draw a picture of yourself.

My name is _____

The color of my eyes is _____

The color of my hair is _____

This is me!

Page 237

I Am Special

1. Color the letters in the word SPECIAL.
2. Cut and paste SPECIAL in the ☐☐☐ below.
3. Color the objects below.
4. Write a story telling why you are special.

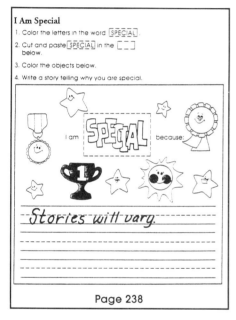

I am SPECIAL because:

Stories will vary.

Page 238

All About Me
Color and write.

Answers will vary.

My name _____

My school _____

My street _____

My phone _____

My city _____

My state _____

Page 239

Birthday Surprise!

1. Complete sentences 1 and 2.
2. Connect the numbers in the dot-to-dot.
3. Color 2 presents red and 3 presents blue.
4. Draw candles on the dot-to-dot picture to show how old you are.
5. Color the dot-to-dot.

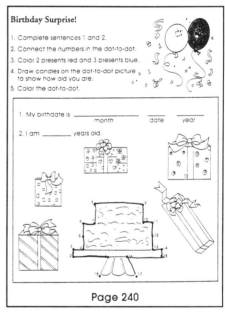

1. My birthdate is _____ month   date   year

2. I am _____ years old.

Page 240

Birthday Bonus Poster

Posters will vary.

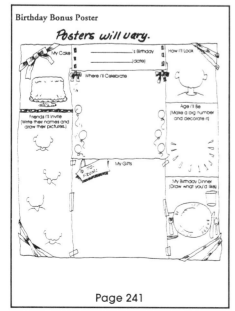

My Cake   ___'s Birthday   How I'll Look
                    (date)

Where I'll Celebrate

Age I'll Be
(Make a big number and decorate it)

Friends I'll Invite
(Write their names and draw their pictures.)

My Gifts

My Birthday Dinner
(Draw what you'd like)

Page 241

Create a Cinquain — A Poem About Me

Line 1 = 1 word
Line 2 = 2 words describing line 1 (adjectives)
Line 3 = 3 action words (ending in ing)
Line 4 = a phrase expressing a feeling or observation about line 1
Line 5 = a word renaming or describing line 1

School
fun, exciting
learning, studying, playing
a great place to be
Elementary

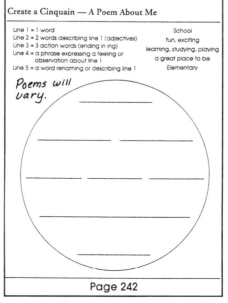

Poems will vary.

Page 242

Feeling Fantastic!

People can have many feelings. They can be happy. They can be sad. Sometimes people can feel angry. Everyone has feelings.

People can have many five. feelings

happy
angry
sad

sad
happy
angry

Make the faces look:
happy   sad   angry

• Draw and color a picture of how you feel.

Page 243

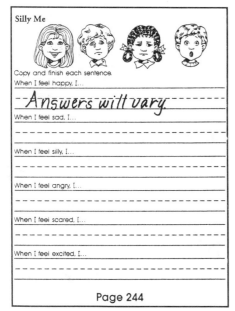

Silly Me

Copy and finish each sentence.

When I feel happy, I...

Answers will vary.

When I feel sad, I...

When I feel silly, I...

When I feel angry, I...

When I feel scared, I...

When I feel excited, I...

Page 244

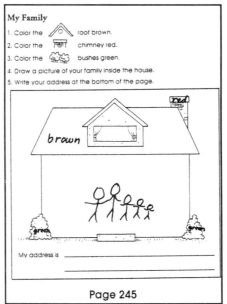

My Family

1. Color the ⌂ roof brown.
2. Color the 🏠 chimney red.
3. Color the 🌳 bushes green.
4. Draw a picture of your family inside the house.
5. Write your address at the bottom of the page.

red

brown

green   green

My address is _____

Page 245

Family Puzzle

Draw family members, pets or fun things you do with your family over the entire puzzle. Color. Cut apart and give the whole puzzle to a classmate to put together.

Puzzles will vary.

Page 246

"My Mom"

Draw a picture of someone in your family.

Pictures and answers will vary.

Write one sentence to tell why this person is special.

Draw a picture of a gift you would like to give this person.

Page 247

Fun with Friends

A friend is someone you like very much. Friends play together. Friends help each other, too. It is nice to have many friends.

friend   from

A *friend* is someone you like.

Yes or No

Friends play together.   (Yes) No
Friends are cars.   Yes (No)
Friends help each other.   (Yes) No

Which are friends?

• Draw and color a picture of you and your friends.

Page 248

Dressed and Ready

1. Draw a picture of you and a friend going to school.
2. Dress you and your friend correctly for the weather.
3. Write your school's name on the sign.

School name

Pictures will vary.

Page 249

Special People

Use the code to name the special people below.

A C D E F G H I L M O P R T
1 2 3 4 5 6 7 8 9 10 11 12 13 14

POLICE
12 11 9 8 2 4
OFFICER
11 5 5 8 2 4 13

DOCTOR
3 11 2 14 11 13

FIRE
5 8 13 4
FIGHTER
5 8 6 7 14 4 13

MAIL
10 1 8 9
CARRIER
2 1 13 13 8 4 13

Page 250

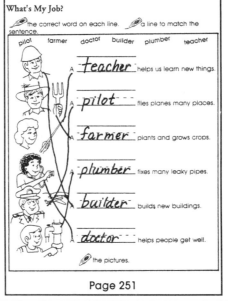

What's My Job?

✏ the correct word on each line. ✏ a line to match the sentence.

pilot   farmer   doctor   builder   plumber   teacher

A *teacher* helps us learn new things.

A *pilot* flies planes many places.

A *farmer* plants and grows crops.

A *plumber* fixes many leaky pipes.

A *builder* builds new buildings.

A *doctor* helps people get well.

✏ the pictures.

Page 251

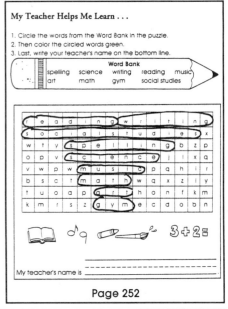

My Teacher Helps Me Learn . . .

1. Circle the words from the Word Bank in the puzzle.
2. Then color the circled words green.
3. Last, write your teacher's name on the bottom line.

Word Bank
spelling science writing reading music
art   math   gym   social studies

r	e	a	d	i	n	g	w	r	i	t	i	n	g
s	o	c	i	a	l	s	t	u	d	i	e	s	x
w	t	y	s	p	e	l	l	i	n	g	b	z	p
o	p	v	s	c	i	e	n	c	e	j	l	x	q
v	w	p	m	u	s	i	c	p	q	h	i	z	
b	s	c	t	m	a	t	h	w	q	x	z	l	y
t	u	o	a	p	g	r	t	h	o	n	f	k	m
k	m	r	s	z	g	y	m	e	c	d	o	b	n

My teacher's name is _____

Page 252

Firefighter Find

A firefighter uses many things in his or her job.

Find the words from the Word Bank in the burning house below.

Word Bank			
boots	hat	oxygen mask	gloves
ax	hose	fire engine	ladder

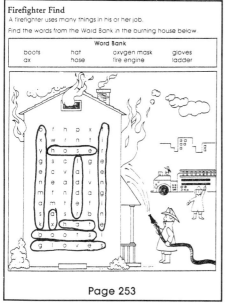

Page 253

In the Cockpit

A pilot is a person who can fly an airplane. A pilot went to a special school to learn to fly a plane. Some pilots fly planes for fun. Some pilots fly planes as their jobs. A pilot sits in a special part of the plane called the cockpit. Have you ever seen a pilot sitting in the cockpit of a plane?

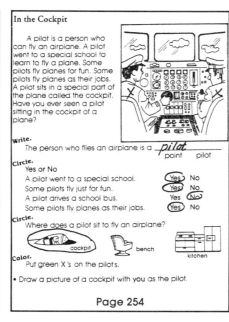

Write.
The person who flies an airplane is a _pilot_
point   pilot

Circle.
Yes or No
A pilot went to a special school.   (Yes) No
Some pilots fly just for fun.   (Yes) No
A pilot drives a school bus.   Yes (No)
Some pilots fly planes as their jobs.   (Yes) No

Circle.
Where does a pilot sit to fly an airplane?
cockpit   bench   kitchen

Color.
Put green X's on the pilots.

• Draw a picture of a cockpit with you as the pilot.

Page 254

On the Farm

Farmers have a very important job. They grow most of the food that we eat. Some farmers grow plants such as oats, corn and wheat. Some farmers raise animals for food. They sell milk from cows. They sell eggs from chickens. Many farmers use machines to help them do their work.

Circle.
I grow (food) flowers trucks for people to eat.
I raise (animals) on my farm.

Check.
What plants do some farmers grow?
☑ oats
☑ corn
☐ steaks
☑ wheat

Match.
Which food comes from which animal?
milk ⟍ chickens
eggs ⟋ cows

Circle the words in the puzzle above.

• Draw a picture of three farm animals.

Page 255

We Care for You

Doctors help many people. They help sick people get well. They help healthy people stay well. People go to special schools to learn to be doctors. There are many kinds of doctors. There are doctors for children, eye doctors, ear doctors, bone doctors and heart doctors. Would you like to be a doctor?

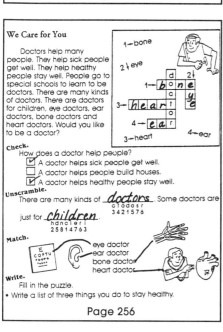

Check.
How does a doctor help people?
☑ A doctor helps sick people get well.
☐ A doctor helps people build houses.
☑ A doctor helps healthy people stay well.

Unscramble.
There are many kinds of _doctors_. Some doctors are
c l o d o s r
3 4 2 1 5 7 6
just for _children_
h d n c l e r l
2 5 8 1 4 7 6 3

Match.
eye doctor
ear doctor
bone doctor
heart doctor

Write.
Fill in the puzzle.

• Write a list of three things you do to stay healthy.

Page 256

Explorers of Space

An astronaut is a person who travels in space. Only a few people can become astronauts. They must be in very good health. They must be very smart. There are special schools to train astronauts. Some astronauts are scientists. Some are pilots. They must work hard to be ready to travel in space.

Unscramble.
A person who travels in space is an _astronaut_
r t n o t s a u d
4 9 6 5 3 2 1 8 7

Check.
☐ Everyone can become an astronaut.
☑ An astronaut must be in very good health.
☑ An astronaut must be very smart.
☑ There are special schools to train astronauts.

Circle.
Some astronauts are: (scientists) judges (pilots)

Color.
Put a red circle around the space words.

• Draw a picture of where you would like to go in space.

Page 257

When I Grow Up . . .

Draw a line to the correct answer.

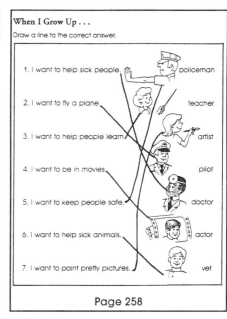

1. I want to help sick people.   policeman
2. I want to fly a plane.   teacher
3. I want to help people learn.   artist
4. I want to be in movies.   pilot
5. I want to keep people safe.   doctor
6. I want to help sick animals.   actor
7. I want to paint pretty pictures.   vet

Page 258

I Want to Be . . .

1. Draw a picture of what you might look like when you grow up.
2. Then write what you want to be when you are grown up and why.

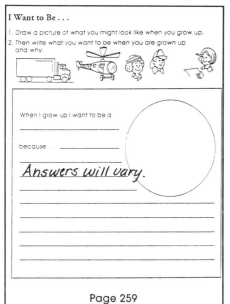

When I grow up I want to be a _____

because _____

Answers will vary.

Page 259

Making a Map

1. Color and cut out the symbols.
2. Paste the symbols next to the matching words in the map key.
3. Then color the rest of the map.

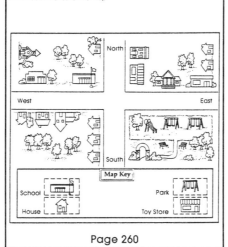

Page 260

A Venice Adventure

1. Start at the gondola, move 2 spaces south. Color the box blue.
2. Go east 2 spaces and draw a brown ⚓ anchor.
3. Go south 2 spaces and put an X in that box.
4. Move one space to the west and draw a red △ in that box.
5. Draw an ⟋ oar in the second box south of the △.
5. Move 2 spaces east to get to the dock at the finish.

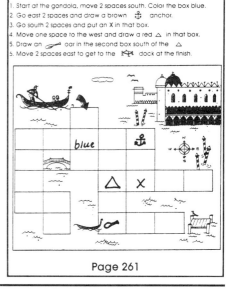

Page 261

Class Map

1. Add some symbols of your own to the map key.
2. Make a map of your classroom using the symbols found in the map key.
3. Add N, S, E, and W to your map.

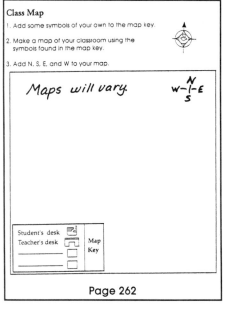

Maps will vary.

Page 262

Nick's Neighborhood

Draw a line along the path Nick used to get home.

1. Nick left the library and stopped to play on the school swings.
2. Next he looked at the puppies in the pet store window.
3. Nick watched as the fire truck raced out of the fire station.
4. Then Nick ran home to get money to buy an ice-cream cone.

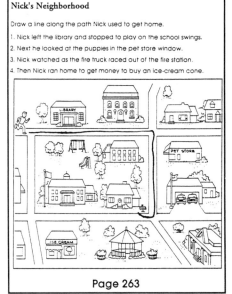

Page 263

Cities, Towns, and Rural Areas

1. Cut and paste the correct signs on each picture.
2. Draw a door on the barn.
3. Draw another tall building in the city.
4. Color the PARK sign yellow.
5. Write where you live in the last picture.
6. Color the pictures.

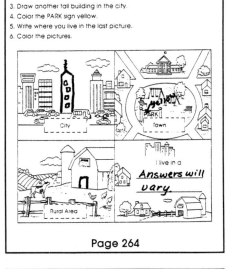

Answers will vary

Page 264

Our State

1. Use a red crayon to outline your state.
2. Color the star yellow and the circle blue.
3. Cut and paste the star where the capital city is located.
4. Cut and paste the circle where your city is located.
5. Complete the sentences below.

This is our state.

Answers will vary.

The name of our state is _____

_____ is our capital city.

The city I live in, or near, is _____

Page 265

Our Country

1. Outline the map green.
2. Color your state blue. Mark an X where you live.
3. Color the rest of the map yellow.
4. Trace the sentence at the bottom in black.

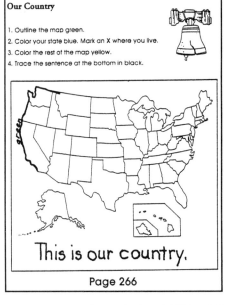

This is our country.

Page 266

Scrambled Continents

Unscramble the words below to spell the continents correctly. Remember to cross out the letters you use. Put in capitals where needed. Use the word bank to help you.

1. rtonh miecara — **North America**
2. cflara — **Africa**
3. eropeu — **Europe**
4. uhots ecaamir — **South America**
5. saia — **Asia**
6. tnrtalacac — **Antarctica**
7. asrulaat — **Australia**

| Africa | Australia | North America | Antarctica |
| Asia | | Europe | South America |

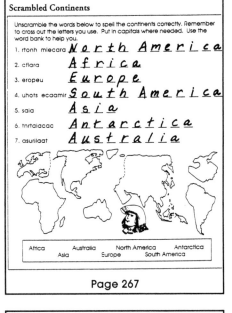

Page 267

Land Ho!

1. Draw a ◯ around the word mountains. Then color the mountains black.
2. Draw a ▢ around the word hills. Then color the hills green.
3. Draw a △ around the word plains. Then color the plains brown.
4. Put an X under the word water. Then color the water blue.

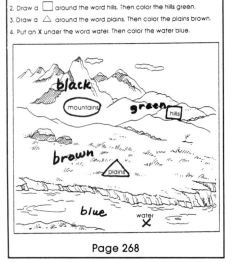

Page 268

Home Rules

1. Number the pictures in the correct order.
2. Then color the pictures.

Keep your room clean.

Be helpful.

Take care of the yard.

Page 269

School Rules

1. Draw a red circle around the good rules.
2. Draw a black X on the bad rules.
3. Then write one of your school rules.

Run in the halls.

Raise your hand in class

Listen when your teacher talks.

Push friends when standing in line.

Talk anytime in class.

Walk in the halls.

Do not push friends when standing in line.

Fight with friends on the playground.

Be noisy in the library.

Be quiet in the library.

Quietly put school things away.

Stand up when riding the school bus.

Throw paper on the floor.

Clean up your lunch area.

One of our school rules is . . . **Answers will vary.**

Page 270

Traffic Signs and Signals

1. Color the STOP sign red.
2. Color the YIELD sign yellow.
3. Do NOT color the DO NOT ENTER sign.
4. Make the TRAFFIC LIGHT green.
5. Color the arrow on the ONE WAY sign black.
6. Color the WALK sign blue.

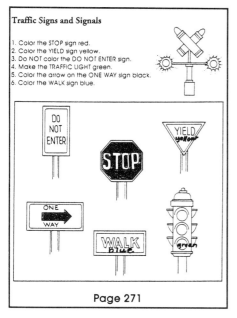

Page 271

Watch Out!
We should always obey safety rules.

1. Draw a black circle around five things that are wrong in the picture.
2. Then color the picture.

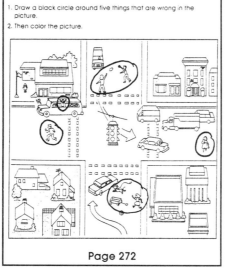

Page 272

Our State's Rules

1. Use the code to complete sentences 1, 2, and 3.
2. Then write your own answers for sentences 4 and 5.

A	C	E	G	I	L	N
1	3	5	7	9	12	14

O	P	R	S	T	V	W
15	16	18	19	20	22	23

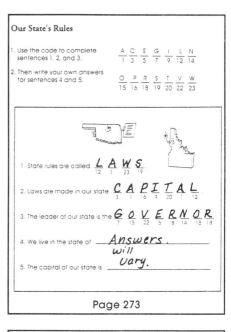

1. State rules are called **L A W S**
2. Laws are made in our state **C A P I T A L**
3. The leader of our state is the **G O V E R N O R**
4. We live in the state of _Answers_
5. The capital of our state is _will vary._

Page 273

Our Nation's Laws

1. Use the Word Bank to write the answers for sentences 1, 2, and 3.
2. Write the name of our nation's President in sentence 4.
3. Draw a picture of our President inside the picture frame.
4. Color the frame and the picture.

Word Bank
President
laws
Washington, D.C.

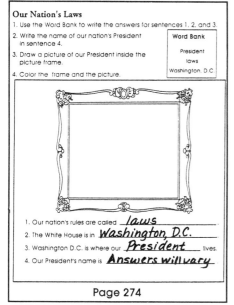

1. Our nation's rules are called _laws_
2. The White House is in _Washington, D.C._
3. Washington D.C. is where our _President_ lives.
4. Our President's name is _Answers will vary_

Page 274

Native American Tribes

1. Color the Indian pictures and the different locations on the map.
2. Cut and paste the pictures correctly on the map.

This is where these Native Americans lived long ago.

Page 275

Native American Homes

1. Write teepee in box 1.
2. Write adobe in box 2.
3. Write wigwam in box 3.
4. Write longhouse in box 4.
5. Draw a sun on the teepee.
6. Color the longhouse brown.
7. Draw a door on the wigwam.
8. Draw small windows on the adobe.

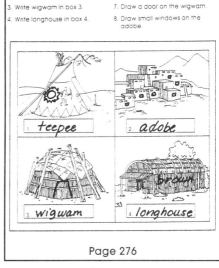

Page 276

Native American Tools

1. Draw a red circle around the corn mortar and the salmon spear.
2. Draw a blue triangle around the digging stick and the fishhook.
3. Draw a green rectangle around the bow and arrow, the canoe paddle, and the hoe.
4. Draw a yellow square around the copper knife and the grinding stones.

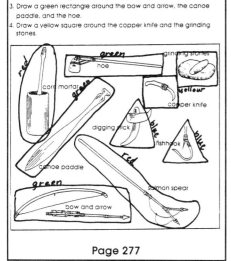

Page 277

The First Thanksgiving
Help the pilgrims find food for their first Thanksgiving.

1. Draw a brown circle around each type of food from the Word Bank hidden in the picture below.
2. Then color the picture.

Word Bank
corn   pumpkin
squash   turkey
onion   beans
berries fish

Page 278

A Whole New World

Write each word on the line next to the matching picture.

Word Bank
berries corn   plant Indian ocean
Pilgrim ship   quail forest turkey

Page 279

Colonial Workers

1. Draw 👞 shoes in the window for the shoemaker.
2. Make some 🥟 dough for the baker to use to make bread.
3. Put a 🔨 hammer in the blacksmith's hand.
4. Draw a 👗 dress on the hanger for the dressmaker.
5. Draw a 🐴 saddle for the saddlemaker.
6. Make sacks of 🌾 flour and 🍬 sugar for the storekeeper.

Page 280

George Washington

1. Connect the dots beginning with number 1.
2. Color the dot-to-dot.
3. On the lines below write:
   George Washington was our first President.

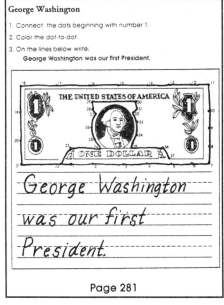

George Washington was our first President.

Page 281

Abraham Lincoln

Word Bank
log cabin
string tie
top hat
White House
ax
books

1. Write the words from the Word Bank under the correct pictures.
2. Then color the pictures.

Abraham Lincoln as a boy — log cabin, ax, books
Abraham Lincoln as President — string tie, top hat, White House

Page 282

Clara Barton

1. Color the medicine bottle brown.
2. Draw a bandage on the man's leg.
3. Color the cross on the wagon red.
4. Color Clara Barton's bag black.
5. Now color the rest of the picture.

Page 283

Martin Luther King, Jr.

1. Color the W's black.
2. Color the X's blue.
3. Color the Y's brown.
4. Color the Z's pink.
5. Color the V's green.

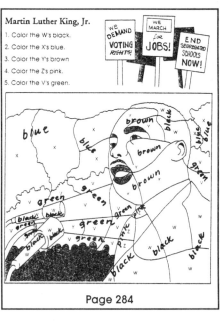

Page 284

Sally Ride

1. Color only the things Sally Ride would need in space.
2. Cut out and paste the colored pictures in the boxes below.
3. Then color Sally Ride.

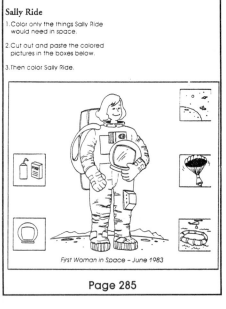

First Woman in Space – June 1983

Page 285

Person I Most Admire

1. Think about the person you most admire.
2. Complete the sentences below.
3. Then draw a picture of yourself with that person.

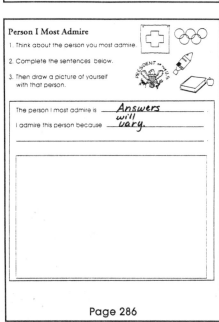

The person I most admire is *Answers*
I admire this person because *will vary.*

Page 286

An African Aunt

1. Read each sentence and write the letter on the ant.
2. Then write each letter in order to find the answer to the riddle at the bottom.

1. Find the ninth letter in crocodile. e
2. Write the first letter in lion. L
3. What is the last letter in giraffe? e
4. Find the middle letter in ape. p
5. What letter is at the end of cheetah? h
6. Write the fifth letter in zebra. a
7. Find the last letter in python. n
8. Write the third letter in ostrich. t

What animal has the biggest aunt?
An e l e p h a n t

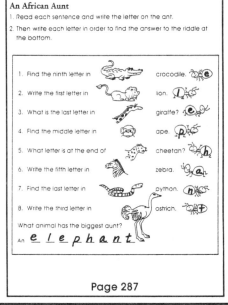

Page 287

Chinese Challenge

Use the Word Bank to write the correct words in the sentences.

Word Bank: Great Wall, bamboo, dragon, panda, jade, rice, City

1. It grows in China and rhymes with "can do."
   b a m b o o
2. Many Chinese stories are written about this monster.
   d r a g o n
3. A beautiful green stone. J a d e
4. This animal could once be found only in China.
   p a n d a
5. Chinese Emperors once lived in the Forbidden C i t y
6. The long wall in China is called the
   G r e a t   W a l l
7. A very important food in the Chinese diet is r i c e

Write the numbered letters in order to find the name of this important city in China.
B e i j i n g
1 2 3 4 5 6 7

Page 288
